*Chess for
the love of it*

To Liddy

A. R. B. Thomas

Chess for
the love of it

Routledge & Kegan Paul
London

First published 1973
by Routledge & Kegan Paul Ltd
Broadway House, 68–74 Carter Lane,
London EC4V 5EL
9 Park Street,
Boston, Mass. 02108, U.S.A.
Printed in Great Britain by
C. Tinling & Co. Ltd, Prescot and London

ISBN 0 7100 7528 6 (C)
ISBN 0 7100 7620 7 (P)

Contents

		page
1	Introduction	1
2	Chess at Cambridge University	7
3	Survey of Recent World Chess	17
4	Meet the Masters	22
5	The Sicilian Defence	37
6	A Few Scalps	48
7	The Möller Defence to the Ruy Lopez	64
8	I Play an American Computer	72
	Index of Openings	81
	Index of Players	82

1 Introduction

What is the fascination of chess? Here are some answers.

For the beginner it is a game, differing only from games like draughts, ludo, halma, etc., in that the rules are rather harder to learn. But once they are mastered, the beginner may have fun.

Next comes the stage when techniques begin to emerge and the beginner realises that there is far more to the game than just having fun. A whole world of logical cause and effect opens up, and the intellect meets a challenge which it will never wholly overcome.

The desire to test one's prowess can then be satisfied by competing in some of the many congresses which take place in this country, and experiencing the peculiar pleasure which comes from utmost endeavour.

But chess is also a team game where one's own result matters little compared with the fortunes of the team, and a player who has an advantage should nevertheless offer a draw if it will give his side victory, but should not accept a draw if it will lose the match. It is a slight criticism of the national grading lists that they tend to make a player think more of himself than of his team.

My father, who was for many years Match Captain of Lancashire and who shared the Lancashire Championship in 1915 with R. W. Houghton, taught me the moves when I was about six years old, and it was some two or three years later that my craving for competitive chess resulted in my arranging a four-round triangular tournament with my father and mother, all the games of which are duly recorded in a notebook. So when the three of us went to Blackpool in 1914 for the Northern Counties Championship, I was present as runner-up in my first important tournament.

A hotel was completely taken over for the congress, and a billiards tournament was arranged for the competitors' wives. I hoped my mother would show greater proficiency at this than at chess; nowadays I should be more concerned for the cloth, which miraculously survived. My own chess clash with Isidor Gunsberg (who, after all, had played a match with Steinitz for the world title) is described in chapter 4, and I thought to find consolation by beating the hotel's page boy at draughts (American checkers), which I knew to be a simple game akin to noughts and crosses. To my utter mortification he beat me every time, even succeeding in 'stalemating' me at an early stage of one of the games, which he claimed won him the game. Nevertheless, the congress had its brighter side for me. Two of the competitors were named Whetstone and Waterhouse. I reflected that they would have been more properly named Whetwater and Stonehouse. Also I recall that the first number of *Chuckles* appeared during the congress. Although I never bought it subsequently, I bought this first number as it was accompanied by a free piece of toffee.

Life at Merchant Taylors' School, Crosby, kept chess interests alive. Half a dozen of the staff played chess in the Common Room, and the Housemaster of the only boarding house was a keen player. The school championship for 1916–17 had sixty boys taking part, roughly one-fifth of the school. The final game was played in the Common Room, with a runner taking the moves to a full classroom where a master gave a commentary. We also played matches against Liverpool Institute, Liverpool College, Manchester Grammar School, Liverpool University, and the Waterloo and Liverpool Chess Clubs (being strengthened in the last three by either masters or old boys), and won a correspondence game with Manchester Grammar School. But on the whole the standard of play was low and not to be compared with some of the chess played in schools today, when between 700 and 800 schools enter for the National Schools Championship.

For my last three years at school I was also a member of the Liverpool Chess Club, which meant more matches and more tournament play. I know that my headmaster was a little dubious about this outside interest, but I just managed an Exhibition to St John's College, Cambridge, in addition to getting my cricket and rugger colours, and being Head of the school. Life, in fact, was very full those days. The First XV, which produced five Internationals in the 1920s, usually played about 28 matches in a season (30 in 1919–20), and the First XI had 20 fixtures. These figures must be almost unbelievable today.

The Liverpool Chess Club was a splendid place! Not only was it open on every weekday, and from morning until late at night, but it had its own kitchen and waitresses to produce delicious steamed fillet of plaice with tea and bread and butter. The clubroom was a spacious affair on the second floor of the Inner Temple, Dale Street, and a section of it was partitioned off for bridge players (who played for 6*d*. a 100). It filled up at midday, nearly emptied in the afternoon, and filled up again at night. Its internationally-known players were P. R. England, Dr H. Holmes and Edmund Spencer, and I never could really decide who was the best of them. Gerald Abrahams joined a little later, and P. F. Blake was an international Problem Composer.

Spencer was nearly always in the club and, if there were no other chess-players present, he might suggest a 'run-round', as he called it. This consisted in putting about sixteen boards of chessmen in a ring (as for a simultaneous exhibition). One player took the outside, the other the inside. The player of white had half a lap start and it was a matter of honour that neither player should catch the other up. Spencer had invented this sport with A. G. Condé, and he was far too good for me at it.

Kriegspiel, lectures, consultation and handicap tournaments were some of the added attractions, and I had the good fortune to win the handicap tournament when the first prize was a magnificent inlaid mahogany table presented by one of the members, Mr J. D. Wright. Spencer had to give me pawn and two moves, and it was nearly twenty-four years later that I discovered that he had resigned unnecessarily. It is extraordinary that nobody noticed it at the time!

The game ended:

	THOMAS	SPENCER
	(*White*)	(*Black*)
28	Q–KKt3	Q–Kt4
29	Q×Q ch.	K×Q
30	P–R5	R–B1
31	P–R6	P×P
32	R×P	R×P
33	P–R4 ch.	K×P
34	R×P	B–Kt4
35	B–Q7	*Resigns*

The high spot of the season was always the ten-board match against Manchester, and I can still recapture the thrill of anticipation as the team assembled for the 2.30 train at Liverpool Central (which arrived at Manchester Central punctually at 3.15), and the pleasure (providing one hadn't lost) of dissecting the games on a travelling chess set coming home. In more recent times I have gone on a trip to Holland with a combined Liverpool–Manchester side. We played against Rotterdam, Luxembourg and The Hague. In 1969 I took part in a four-club contest between The Hague, Glasgow, Manchester and Liverpool, played in Liverpool.

Match chess has always appealed to me, and I must have played in about 80 county matches, 17 for Lancashire and the rest for Devon. My proudest moment was in the Final of the English Counties Championship in 1935, when my draw as Black against the British Champion, W. Winter, won the match for Lancashire. My saddest moment was in 1954, when I was asked by the British Chess Federation whether I should be available to play in Buenos Aires as a member of the British team and my headmaster would not give me leave of absence. My wretched performance at the following Hastings Congress was a consequence of this.

Chess problems form a separate branch of the game and problem-composition can be quite a considerable art. I have no skill at it, but claim that good players can usually solve problems. To justify this claim, I entered for the 100th problem-solving competition run by Brian Harley in the *Observer* and was 100 per cent successful (competing under the name of Billy Budd!). In solving problems, I learned to appreciate how beautiful were many of the compositions.

Correspondence chess is another way of enjoying the game and is well-organised in this country. My annual game in the Counties Correspondence Championship usually takes up about six months of the year. I hope still to be playing correspondence chess in extreme old age!

Of tournament chess, which has proliferated so much recently, I would recall with great affection the many Hastings Christmas Congresses where most of the world's greatest players have taken part. I have notched up over 100 points at Hastings (either in the Premier Tournament or the one immediately below it) and also in the British Championship. My first Hastings Congress was in 1922–3 (as the guest of J. A. J. Drewitt, that lovable, eccentric don) and I enjoyed playing fifty years later. Together with a host of other chess players I should like to thank warmly the various organisers of chess at Hastings.

Finally, I have the belief that certain games of chess are inherently beautiful and give much the same kind of aesthetic satisfaction as well-played music. I like to think that many of the games in this book have this quality. That is one reason why I have not overwhelmed them with notes, and have refrained almost entirely from the customary '!' and '?' and '?!'. It could well be argued that I am not being sufficiently objective or self-critical, and that the mistakes should all be pinpointed. I will admit this, but comfort myself by thinking how much satisfaction the reader will obtain by searching for them himself. Also I wonder what benefit there would be in advocating certain lines of play (especially against the Sicilian Defence), while at the same time revealing how they could best be defeated.

When I played the M.I.T. computer in America, I felt that this belief in beauty was also on trial, and said so to my American friends. 'Oh, we shall soon programme beauty into it,' they replied. I hope not, while admitting that certain beautiful ideas of the past are well-known techniques of today.

I should like to close this introduction by giving the game which won the Boyd Prize for the best game played in the Counties Correspondence Championship for 1971. It is a little gem.

White: R. J. G. Bird (Worcestershire)
Black: P. E. Walker (Somerset)

1 P–K4	P–K3	At this stage the postal strike
2 P–Q4	P–Q4	intervened, and White ruminated
3 Kt–QB3	B–Kt5	on what seemed to him to be a
4 P–K5	P–QB4	lost game.
5 P–QR3	B × Kt ch.	17 B × Kt	Kt × P
6 P × B	Q–B2	18 P × Kt	Q × Kt ch.
7 Q–Kt4	K–B1	19 K–B2	Q × R
8 Kt–K2	Kt–K2	20 B–B5 ch.	K–Kt1
9 B–Q2	QKt–B3	We have now reached the
10 P–KR4	P–KR4	position which is shown on the
11 Q–Kt5	Kt–B4	following page.
12 P–Kt4	P × KKtP	Miraculously White mates
13 Q × P (Kt4)	B–Q2	his opponent in, at most, nine
14 P–R5	P × P	moves. Is not chess a lovely
15 P–KB4	P × P	game?
16 Kt × P	Kt–K6	

2 Chess at Cambridge University

The origins of chess at our senior universities, together with detailed results of all the matches played between them from 1873 to 1934, have been so fully given by P. W. Sergeant in *A Century of British Chess* that a separate chapter here may seem superfluous.

But at a time when Cambridge has won the Centenary Match, when Cambridgeshire (almost entirely composed of University players) has won the English Counties Championship for three successive years, and when Cambridge University has won the National Club Championship three times between 1969 and 1972 (and six times in all), the subject gains in importance and a comparison between the present and the past may not be without interest.

The first Oxford–Cambridge chess match was played in 1873 on the eve of the Boat Race to which *The Times* had been devoting a couple of columns for many days past. This chess match passed unnoticed in *The Times* until 1874, when it was referred to in a fairly full account of the second match, also played on the eve of the Boat Race. Both these matches were played at the City of London Chess Club in their rooms at the City Restaurant, Milk Street, Cheapside. Play lasted from 6 p.m. until 11 p.m., and the players (seven-a-side) might play as many games as they could fit in, any unfinished games being adjudicated by Steinitz, who was then World Champion. The average number of games between the players was just under three.

The rooms were festooned in light and dark blue and, to alleviate the pressure on the teams (the spectators, according to *The Times*, numbered about 800), two other rooms were in use, in one of which Zukertort played six games simultaneously blindfold and, in the other, Blackburne gave a simultaneous exhibition against seven opponents who were regularly replaced as their games ended. At the conclusion of play and after the adjudications by Steinitz the two teams were entertained to a repast by the City of London Club.

Falconer Madan, who played for Oxford in both these matches, was present at the dinner which followed the fiftieth match, and I regret that I didn't ask him for his memories. But the *B.C.M.* for March 1973 contains a splendid account of the first match, together with an exciting Ponziani played on top board. The remaining openings employed were the Scotch, Petroff, Sicilian, French, Queen's Gambit and Queen's Fianchetto.

I was at Cambridge from 1923 to 1926 and chess occupied a good deal of my time. I won the University Championship three times and noted that the only players who had done this previously were H. E. Atkins and C. E. C. Tattersall. Since then C. H. O'D. Alexander has won it four times, but no one else has won it outright three times, although today the leading players do not compete.

But the university matches were another story. In 1924 I reached the following position after making a dreadful blunder:

The game ended: 59 Q–Kt5 ch., K–B7; 60 Q–Q2 ch., K–Kt6. It was clear I had a draw. Unfortunately the match score was Oxford 3½, Cambridge 2½. If I took the draw the match was lost. So I had to give my opponent a chance to blunder. 61 K–Q4 (To this day I do not know whether to be proud or ashamed of this move; on balance, I think, I'm proud of it.), Q–Kt8 ch.; 62 K–Q3, Q–B8 ch.; 63 K–B3, Q–B6 ch. and White resigned.

A. OPPENHEIM (*Black*)

THOMAS (*White*)

Later in the year I played in a Cable Match between the English and American universities.

In my second year I was Secretary and took the opportunity to double the fixture list for the following year. For the record, we played and beat Imperial (twice), Cambridge Town (twice), Hastings, West London, Ipswich, North London (twice), the Northern Universities, the Reform Club; we drew with Insurance and United Banks; we lost to United Banks and Hampstead, 15 matches altogether. But the Oxford match was again lost, and my Cambridge

Springs Defence held no problems for G. S. A. Wheatcroft. He thoroughly outplayed me, and I seem to recall having heard that he had been coached by T. H. Tylor. The Cambridge lead in the series, which had been held since 1879, was nearly wiped out and the score stood at 23–22, with four matches tied.

When I became President in my third year, the fiftieth match loomed ahead, with the awful prospect of a sixth successive Oxford win putting them level. Everything had to be done to prevent this. W. Winter (who had been President in 1919, when Cambridge won 7—0, and was later to win the British Championship twice) came as my guest for a week and gave three magnificent lectures (which I copied out and still retain) on the Sicilian Defence; the Slav Defence; and the general lines of attack for White in the Queen's Gambit.

Finally, I took one other element of the match into consideration. It has always been a seven-board affair, which means that one side has four Whites to the other side's three. I decided that the best way to offset the disadvantage of losing the toss would be to have players at boards 2, 4 and 6 who would really appreciate being White.

When the day came we did in fact lose the toss, but only board 6 smashed home for us. Victor Coates on board 4 accepted a draw, which made victory certain, when he had a great advantage. This time I managed to hold Wheatcroft to a draw and our only loss was board 2. We won the match 4½—2½. Perhaps the most interesting game was this one on board 5. It also shows the effect of Winter's coaching. Instead of his dashing 22nd move, White should simply have played 22 Kt–Kt5.

A. W. STONIER (OXFORD)			
J. A. HERRICK (CAMBRIDGE)			

#	White / Black	#	White / Black
1	P–Q4 / P–Q4	2	Kt–KB3 / Kt–KB3
3	P–B4 / P–B3	4	Kt–B3 / P×P
5	P–K3 / P–QKt4	6	P–QR4 / P–Kt5
7	Kt–R2 / P–K3	8	B×P / QKt–Q2
9	0–0 / B–Kt2	10	Q–K2 / P–B4
11	P–QKt3 / B–K2	12	B–Kt2 / 0–0
13	KR–Q1 / Q–Kt3	14	Kt–B1 / P–QR4
15	Kt–Q3 / KR–Q1	16	QR–B1 / B–Q3
17	P×P / Kt×P	18	B–Q4 / QR–B1
19	QKt–K5 / Q–B2	20	B×Kt / B×B
21	R×R ch. / Q×R	22	Kt×BP / K×Kt

23 $\dfrac{\text{Kt–Kt5 ch.}}{\text{K–K2}}$ 24 $\dfrac{\text{Kt} \times \text{KP}}{\text{Q–Q3}}$ 25 $\dfrac{\text{Kt} \times \text{P}}{\text{Q–K4}}$ 26 $\dfrac{\text{Kt–K6}}{\text{B–Q3}}$

27 $\dfrac{\text{P–B4}}{\text{Q} \times \text{Kt}}$ 28 $\dfrac{\text{B} \times \text{Q}}{\text{R} \times \text{R ch.}}$ 29 $\dfrac{\text{K–B2}}{\text{Kt–K5 ch.}}$ *Resigns*

The match was played at the City of London Chess Club in Wardrobe Court, near to St Paul's. It was played on a Friday towards the end of a week in which the two universities (past and present members included) had combined to play London University, Insurance, Hampstead, the City of London, West London and the Reform Club. All these matches were won and the City of London (then England's premier club) was really quite a notable scalp.

On the Saturday both sides combined for a seven-course Jubilee Dinner at the Trocadero Restaurant. Thirty of us were present and the Guest of Honour was H. E. Atkins. As stated earlier, Falconer Madan was also there. I still have the menu, autographed by all present.

Later that year Wheatcroft and I were two of the twelve selected to play in a rather weak British Championship. We each scored five points (out of eleven) and drew our individual game once again. But, if asked to compare the standards of university chess in 1926 with those of today, I should immediately plump for today. Far more juniors play the game and consequently the universities have strength in depth. In my time a university side could no more have taken on a strong county side in a 16-board match than England could do the same with Russia at the present time.

Today the Cambridge fixture list includes eight county and eight club matches in addition to National Club events. Oxford are played four times as, in addition to the traditional match, the second and third teams and freshmen do battle. For the last thirteen years the club has produced its own magazine, *Dragon*, from whose latest editorial I quote: 'The good old British maxim "Individual selfishness leads to the common good" has a particular significance for chess players.'

To illustrate present standards of play I should like to give two games. The first won the Best Game Prize in the Freshmen's Tournament, 1969; the second was played in the 1970–1 Counties Championship and is taken, with notes by the winner, from *Dragon*, Summer 1971. Also worthy of mention is the pretty game won by A. W.

Williams against M. J. Corden in the 1970 varsity match. It can be found in *British Chess Magazine,* May 1970.

White: B. Rothbart
Black: A. H. Williams

1 P–K4	P–QB4
2 Kt–KB3	P–Q3
3 P–Q3	Kt–QB3
4 P–KKt3	P–KKt3
5 B–Kt2	B–Kt2
6 0–0	Kt–B3
7 Kt–R3	0–0
8 Kt–B4	P–QKt4
9 Kt–K3	R–Kt1
10 Kt–R4	B–Q2
11 P–KB4	P–QR4
12 P–KKt4	P–R5
13 R–Kt1	Kt–K1
14 P–Kt5	P–Kt5
15 P–B5	Kt–K4
16 R–B4	Kt–B2
17 Kt–B3	P–Kt6
18 RP×P	RP×P
19 P–B3	B–QB3
20 Kt–Kt4	Kt×Kt
21 R×Kt	P–Q4
22 P–K5	P×P
23 R–KR4	Kt–K3
24 B–R3	R–K1
25 B×P	Kt–B1

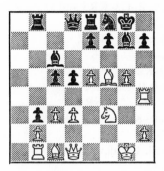

26 Kt–Q4   . . . . .

The onslaught begins. Black defends valiantly but to no avail.

26	P×Kt
27 Q–R5	Q–Kt3
28 B×P ch.	Kt×B
29 Q×Kt ch.	K–B1
30 P–Kt6	P×P dis. ch.
31 K–Kt2	P–Q5 dis. ch.
32 K–B2	B–K5
33 B–R6	P–K3
34 Q×B ch.	K–K2
35 Q×P ch.	K–Q1
36 B–Kt5 ch.	K–B1
37 Q×R ch.	*Resigns*

White: A. J. Oddie (Cambridgeshire)
Black: J. Cook (Hertfordshire)

1 P–K4	P–QB4		5 Kt–QB3	Kt–B3
2 Kt–KB3	P–Q3		6 B–QB4	P–K3
3 P–Q4	P×P			
4 Kt×P	Kt–KB3			

This was the first open Sicilian I had played for six

B

years. At lunch on the day of the match I was instructed by A. H. Williams on how to deal with this system ('Develop your lumps, play P–KKt4–Kt5, Q–R5, R–Q3–KR3 and Q×RP mate').

7 B–Kt3	B–K2
8 B–K3	0–0
9 Q–K2	P–QR3
10 0–0–0	Kt×Kt
11 B×Kt	Q–R4
12 KR–Kt1	P–QKt4
13 P–Kt4	....

Well, I've developed all my lumps!

| 13 .... | P–Kt5 |
| 14 P–Kt5 | Kt–K1 |

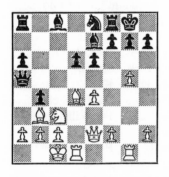

15 Q–R5	P×Kt
16 R–Q3	P–K4
17 B×BP	Q–B2

If 17 ...., P–Kt3 first, then 18 Q–R6, Q–B2; 19 P–B4 (threat P–B5, R–R3 and Q×P mate), 19 ...., P×P; 20 B–R4, B–Q2; 21 R–R3, B×R; 22 B×Kt, P–B3; 23 B×P, B–Q1; 24 P×P and mates.

| 18 P–Kt6 | P×P |

If 18 ...., Kt–B3; 19 Q–Kt5.

19 R×KtP	R–Kt1
20 QR–Kt3	R×B
21 R–R6	P–Kt3

Or first 21 ...., B–Kt4 ch.; 22 R×B, P–Kt3; 23 R–R8 ch., K–Kt2; 24 Q–R6 ch., K–B3; 25 R×P ch., P×R; 26 Q×R ch., Q–B2; 27 Q×Q ch., K×Q; 28 BP×R and White's surfeit of rooks and pawns should prove decisive.

| 22 KR×P ch. | P×R |
| 23 Q×P ch. | *Resigns* |

In reply to a letter of mine, R. D. Keene very kindly wrote to me:

One of the reasons for our strength is that the concentration of good players here encourages others to apply to Cambridge, and thus we have a self-perpetuating system.

Other contributory causes: frequent analytical sessions and exchange of ideas amongst the leading players, plus great determination and fine team spirit in County and National Club matches. You can gauge the activity of the club from the fixture card, but we also have two inter-college competitions (league and knock-out) and non-scheduled county matches which don't appear on the fixture card since they are played in the third term. As an example of team spirit, we aways try to field our very strongest team in National Club Championship even against weak opposition in the early rounds. This is a matter of principle.

One recent success: [in November 1971] Cambridge won the National Team Lightning (10-second) Championship, held at Slough. This was the first time we had entered.

In conclusion, I would like to say that we are all very conscious of being the strongest club in Britain, and this means we try a lot harder all the time in order to maintain our status. This factor also helps to inspire players who are competing in individual events; they are representatives of Cambridge and therefore they must succeed.

P.S.   My theory is that strength breeds strength; strong players attract other good players and the mutual exchange of ideas plus tough competition forces all the standards up.

Another example is my old school, Dulwich College. When I was a new boy in 1960, the school was a chess nonentity; by the time I left in 1966, we had won the National Schools Championship twice and we dominated the London Schools and Kent Schools Leagues.

Since I left Dulwich strength has, if anything, increased and there is now a thriving Old Boys' Club as well. For examples: [In 1971] two Dulwich players (one a schoolboy, the other at Oxford) jointly won the Southern Counties Championship; five Dulwich players were in [the 1971] Senior British Championship; [in 1970] three Dulwich pupils tied for first in the British Under-18 Championship; at least six Dulwich boys have played for England in international representative events.

Since I came to Cambridge a similar pattern has re-enacted itself here. I shouldn't like it to appear that I am saying that I was somehow miraculously responsible for the rise in strength at both school and university; I'm merely pointing out that I was twice involved in typical 'strength breeds strength' situations. At both Dulwich and Cambridge I was always in the company of many other good players.

1971 was indeed a peak year for Cambridge chess when R. D. Keene won the British Championship and W. R. Harston came third (tying with Howard Williams, also of Cambridge). It was fitting that these two led the British team which inflicted a somewhat rare defeat on the Netherlands in October of the same year. Neither should it be forgotten that Mrs Hartston won the British Ladies' Championship for the second year in succession.

I should like to give here the memorable game which virtually decided the men's championship, with some of Keene's notes from the *British Chess Magazine*.

White: Dr J. Penrose
Black: R. D. Keene

1 P–K4	P–KKt3
2 P–Q4	B–Kt2
3 Kt–QB3	P–Q3
4 P–B4	Kt–KB3
5 Kt–B3	0–0
6 B–Q3	Kt–B3
7 P–KR3	....

A new idea at this stage. White stops Black playing B–KKt5, and also prepares P–KKt4. However it does represent a slight loss of time and Black can employ this respite to inaugurate a swift counter-attack on the Queen's side.

7	Kt–QKt5

Ogling White's KB and preparing the undermining advance . . . ., P–QB4. If now 8 B–K2 then P–QB4; 9 P×P, Kt–R4; 10 P×P, Kt–Kt6; 11 P×P, Q×P; 12 R–KKt1, R–Q1 and Black wins. This variation exposes one of the seamy sides of 7 P–KR3, i.e. the weakness of the KKt3 square.

8 B–K3	P–Kt3

This helps to support . . . .,

P–QB4; also a path is cleared to QR3 for the Black QB. This factor soon becomes of great importance.

9 P–R3	Kt×B ch.
10 P×Kt	P–B4
11 Q–Q2	B–QR3
12 K–B2	....

A much saner procedure is 12 0–0. The text plans the grandiose operation QR–KKt1, P–KKt4, P–KR4, but it is much too cumbersome to be realistic in the circumstances and, already on the very next move, White is forced into a dismal retreat.

12	R–B1

This defeats all White's aggressive intentions. If now 13 QR–KKt1 then 13 . . . ., P–B5; 14 P × P, R × P threatening both R × Kt and Q–R1, when White's centre folds up.

13 KR–QB1   Kt–Q2

Intending . . . ., P × P and . . . ., Kt–B4, hence

14 P–Q5   P–K3
14 P × P   P × P
16 R–K1   . . . .

White's position is near critical. Now, or on move 17, he had to play K–Kt1.

16 . . . .   Kt–B3
17 QR–Q1   . . . .

17 K–Kt is absolutely imperative. 17 P–Q4 (perhaps planned with 16 R–K1) is quite unplayable: 17 . . . ., P × P; 18 B × P (if 18 Kt × P, R × Kt), P–K4; 19 P × P, P × P; 20 B × P, Kt–Kt5 ch. and wins.

17 . . . .   P–Q4

This leads to a win virtually by force, and there is little else to comment on. White meets each direct threat, as it arises, until his resources are no longer sufficient to cope.

18 P × P   P × P
19 P–Q4   . . . .

Else Black wins with . . . ., P–Q5.

19 . . . .   Kt–K5 ch.
20 Kt × Kt   P × Kt
21 Kt–K5   P–KKt4

22 K–Kt1   P × BP
23 B × P   Q × P ch.
24 Q × Q   P × Q
25 P–KKt3   . . . .

Or 25 R × KP, R × B followed by . . . ., B × Kt.

25 . . . .   KR–K1

Compare the two diagrams—'Before and After'. Now the centre is all Black's. In regaining his pawn, White gets into a fearful tangle. The concluding moves were:

26 KR × P   R–B4
27 QR–K1   P–Q6
28 Kt–B3   R × R
29 R × R   B–Kt2
30 R–K3   P–Q7
31 Kt × P   B–Q5
32 K–B1   B–R3 ch.
33 K–Kt2   B × R
34 B × B   R–B7
35 P–Kt3   B–Kt2 ch.
36 K–B1   B–Q4
37 K–K1   B × P
    Resigns

For the record Table 1 gives the Oxford–Cambridge results since

1935. *A Century of British Chess* shows that, up to then, Cambridge had won 26 matches to Oxford's 25 and seven had been drawn. Oxford led in the series in 1965 for the first time since 1877. In 1972 Cambridge led 38—35 with 17 matches drawn.

Table 1. *Results in the Oxford v. Cambridge Universities annual chess match, 1935–72*

Year	C.	O.	Year	C.	O.	Year	C.	O.
1935	3½—3½		1951	3½—3½		1962	2½—4½	
1936	6 —1		1952	4½—2½		1963	3 —4	
1937	4 —3		1953	2 —5		1964	3½—3½	
1938	3 —4		1954	3½—3½		1965	1½—5½	
1939	4 —3		1955	4 —3		1966	3½—3½	
1940*			1956	3 —4		1967	5½—1½	
1946	2½—4½		1957	3½—3½		1968	5 —2	
1947	3½—3½		1958	5½—1½		1969	2½—4½	
1948	1½—5½		1959	3½—3½		1970	4 —3	
1949	1 —6		1960	3½—3½		1971	5 —2	
1950	4½—2½		1961	3½—3½		1972	5½—1½†	

* Unofficial matches were played during the Second World War. Of these, Oxford won two, Cambridge one, and two were drawn.

† In 1973 the Centenary Match was won 4–3 by Cambridge.

3   *Survey of Recent World Chess*

Today we see in chess the fight of aspiring Americanism against the old European intellectual life: a struggle between the technique of Capablanca, a virtuoso in whose play one can find nothing tangible to object to, and between great European masters, all of them artists, who have the qualities as well as the faults of artists in the treatment of the subject they devote their lives to: they experimentalise and in striving after what is deep down, they overlook what is near at hand. . . .

Yet they go on investigating and building further. Who will come out of this struggle victorious? Nobody can prophesy the answer. But one thing is certain. If Americanism is victorious in chess, it will also be so in life. For in the idea of chess and the development of the chess mind we have a picture of the intellectual struggle of mankind.

So wrote Richard Reti in 1923 in his magnificent book, *Modern Ideas in Chess*. Capablanca was then world champion and his overthrow seemed unimaginable. Yet it occurred but four years later in the most gruelling battle of all time. Alekhine, who was a Russian *émigré*, was the challenger, and the title was to go to the one who first scored six wins. The match opened sensationally as Alekhine won the first game, but after ten games had been played Capablanca led by 2—1, with seven games drawn. Then Alekhine won the eleventh and twelfth games, and after twenty games was leading 3—2, with fifteen games drawn. Ten games more were played, and after 30 games Alekhine was still leading 4—3 with 23 drawn games. It seemed the match would be interminable, but suddenly Capablanca cracked and Alekhine won 6—3, with 25 of the 34 games drawn.

The strain on both players must have been exceedingly great and a return match never took place. Instead, Alekhine defended his title successfully twice against Bogoljubow, lost it in 1935 to the great Dutch player Euwe only to regain it in 1937 through the graciousness of his opponent in allowing a return match. The Second World War prevented any further matches taking place, and Alekhine died soon after it was over. His games are preserved in two books he annotated himself, entitled *My Best Games of Chess*, and in a third book, *Alekhine's Best Games of Chess 1938–1945*, beautifully produced by C. H. O'D. Alexander, who wrote of them, 'These games are the product of the life of a man of genius . . . [who] was one of the very greatest players who has ever lived, and his games have a beauty and fascination entirely of their own.'

When Alekhine died (in March 1946) the international chess federation (FIDE) took over the organisation of the world championship. In 1948 it organised a tournament which Botvinnik won and thus became world champion. Periodically the world champion has to defend his title in a 24-game match against a challenger who is the survivor of a most gruelling ordeal. Zonal tournaments are succeeded by an inter-zonal tournament and after this eight survivors knock each other out in a series of matches. First there are four survivors, then two, and only then the challenger. After 1948 the Russians monopolised the world championship with Botvinnik, Smyslov, Tal, Petrosian and Spassky holding the title.

In 1970 a 10-board, 4-round match was played between Russia and the Rest of the World. Leading the Rest of the World were Bent Larsen of Denmark with many brilliant tournament successes to his credit, and Bobby Fischer, the young American genius. Although Russia won the match by 20½ to 19½, the main excitement was that Larsen held his own with Spassky, and Fischer beat Petrosian by 3—1. I was in South America at the time and the match occupied half the front page of the newspapers. People kept coming to me to say that Fischer had beaten Petrosian in their first game, and that he had done it again in the second. It was sensational news!

So the 1971 matches to determine the challenger to Spassky were of tremendous interest, the favourites being Larsen, Fischer, Petrosian and Korchnoi.

All four won their first-round matches, Fischer defeating Taimanov by the unbelievable score of 6—0. Now Fischer had to play Larsen, and Petrosian Korchnoi. Once again the impossible happened and Fischer won 6—0. These two match results of Fischer have no parallel in chess history, and the chess world could hardly wait for his match with Petrosian, who had reached the final by drawing all the games in his two matches save for one in each, which he won.

Fischer and Petrosian met in Buenos Aires in October 1971. Fischer won the first game, but at last he was partially stopped. Petrosian won the second game and the next three were drawn. It seemed a close contest. But it wasn't! Fischer again did the impossible by winning the next four games for the match. That he could do this against the acknowledged greatest exponent of defensive technique is something which will be remembered by chess players for all time.

When the match for the world title itself took place in Reykjavic during July and August 1972, between Spassky and Fischer, many months of involved negotiations had preceded it, and the day fixed for the first game had passed with Fischer still in America and apparently likely to stay there. At this stage Mr J. D. Slater, who has done much to help chess financially in this country, offered to double the prize money. As he explained in a letter to me:

When I heard that Fischer was not going to play against Spassky I was very disappointed as I had been looking forward to the match. I also knew that many other chess players all over the world would be disappointed. I did not think that it was just money that was holding Fischer back, but thought he had a psychological problem. I felt therefore that the double challenge of the extra money and the suggestion that he might be frightened of Spassky was the right gambit. It certainly seems to have worked!

The match started shortly after this, a week or so late. Fischer won the 3rd, 5th, 6th, 8th, 10th, 13th, 21st (and last) games; Spassky won the 1st, 2nd (by default) and 11th; the remaining eleven (including a run of seven from the 14th to the 20th) were drawn. Some of the chess was strikingly original and beautiful, some was marred by elementary blunders. We are all indebted to Dr Max Euwe for his arduous labours before the match started, to Boris Spassky for his sportsmanship in the face of almost unbearable disappointments, and to Bobby Fischer for his chess genius. Richard Reti's wheel has come full circle; again we see 'the fight of aspiring Americanism'. May we also see a worthy champion!

As yet there is no sign of England producing a player capable of challenging for the world title. England's greatness in chess was in the nineteenth century and lingered on in the Edwardian age. Cable matches between Great Britain and America begun in 1896 were played annually (except for the years 1904–6) until Britain's third successive success in 1911 brought the series to an end, each side having won six matches and drawn one. Since 1911 English chess has had no such comparable success.

England regularly competes in the Chess Olympiads, in the Clare-Benedict Tourney (confined to West European countries), and plays annual matches with Holland—all with indifferent success.

Why should this be so? Today in England there are far more congresses than ever before, there are far, far more youngsters playing the game, and coaching schemes abound. Why then does the national team give such a moderate account of itself?

The answer, above all others, is that the climate of opinion does nothing to help. England is not, in fact, a chess-minded country. The great cities do not have their many chess centres where the game is played and discussed from morning to night. It should surely come as a shock to the present generation to learn that the early matches, from 1873 onwards, between Oxford and Cambridge Universities were played before audiences variously estimated at from 400 to 700 (*A Century of British Chess*).

Again, the reporting of chess matches and congresses, both in the press and on radio and television, is feeble compared with fifty years ago when the results of Saturday's county matches were put on the London train to ensure their appearing in *The Times* on Monday, with full details of the individual results. Today it is difficult enough to find club or county results in *Chess* or the *British Chess Magazine*. It is hopeless to look for them in the national press.

Finally, the selection and training of teams to represent this country is a thoroughly amateur affair, which would be radically altered by a public which really cared. I had the misfortune to be a member of the BCF Selection Committee a few years ago, but was so appalled by the inadequacy of proceedings I felt powerless to remedy that I resigned quite quickly. Basically, I felt the Selection Committee did not meet often enough and spent too little time on the job when it did meet; it treated far too lightly the appointment of a Team Captain and the consideration of the powers he should be given; it neglected any idea of a Team Training Programme; it thought in terms of the future and not of the present. The picture would not, however, be complete without my balancing these severe strictures by paying a sincere tribute to the many dedicated men who selflessly work to improve British chess.

For some years the BCF has done an excellent job in encouraging chess among the young, but the best national side would have the correct blend of youth and experience. British teams need to be picked to win the match immediately ahead, not to gain experience for a future match. Then we should not have the absurdity of a British Champion being passed over on the grounds that he was too old.

But the basic trouble remains the climate of opinion which is not strong enough to insist that things should be done properly, and that there should be a truly professional approach. In 1970 I had the pleasure of playing chess in Colombia. In the city of Medellin there were four or five cafés where chess players were queuing up from morning to night to play at one of the twenty-five chess tables. The form of the leading Colombian chess players was well-known and much discussed, so that it was no surprise to me that this small country finished ahead of England in the 1970 Chess Olympiad.

Perhaps the day when this country will take its rightful place in the chess world is nearer at hand than I imagine. We do not lack for enthusiastic amateurs, but we need the dedicated professional approach. English chess needs its own Sir Alf Ramsey.

4 *Meet the Masters*

Meet the Masters was the title given to an excellent chess book published over thirty years ago. *Masters of the Chess Board*, by Reti, was published earlier still. I shall keep the title, although conscious that masters nowadays are divided into separate categories —grand, international and national.

The first master I met was Isidor Gunsberg, at the Northern Counties Chess Congress at Blackpool in 1914. Gunsberg easily won the Open Tournament and gave a simultaneous display at which I was one of his opponents. I was quite disappointed when my father resigned the game for me, as I was only a knight and a few pawns down at the time.

Gunsberg was a small man who, in the nineteenth century, operated from the inside a chess automaton, under the name of Mephisto. I suspect his automaton played better chess than today's computer.

The next chess master I encountered was Capablanca, when he made a tour of England in the autumn of 1919. He gave thirty-six simultaneous displays, taking on about forty opponents each time. His figures were incredible as he played 1382 games, winning 1280, drawing 72 and losing only 30. His most disastrous result was at Waterloo, which is a suburb of Liverpool. Here he lost three games and drew one. The losses were to myself and to my father and to our great friend, Mr S. R. Jopson. He drew with Capt. Bustin, but, according to Mr Jopson who was sitting next to him, Capablanca would have lost this game also if the gallant captain had not insisted on playing an occasional move of his own instead of doing as he was told.

Capablanca was, on this occasion, a guest of the Liverpool Chess Club, and was alleged to have told his host that the Albin Counter Gambit was the best way of dealing with the Queen's Gambit if White played 2 P–QB4 instead of 2 Kt–KB3. Nowadays I find it very difficult to believe that he could have said this, but my authority at the time seemed impeccable.

The next time I met Capablanca was at the great London Congress of 1922 when I played him in the Lightning Tournament. He didn't take long to polish me off and, as there was a little time before the next round, I thought I would ask him about the Evans Gambit Declined in which I was then interested. Accordingly I made on the board the moves $1 \frac{\text{P–K4}}{\text{P–K4}}$ $2 \frac{\text{Kt–KB3}}{\text{Kt–QB3}}$ $3 \frac{\text{B–B4}}{\text{B–B4}}$ $4 \frac{\text{P–QKt4}}{\text{B–Kt3}}$ $5 \frac{\text{P–Kt5}}{\text{Kt–R4}}$ $6 \frac{\text{Kt}\times\text{P.}}{}$ The text-books gave a choice of Kt–R3, Q–B3 and Q–Kt4 for Black, and I was about to ask Capablanca which he preferred when he pushed the position away. Two years latei I asked Rubinstein the same question and, although he didn't speak English, he indicated Kt–R3 and spent some time looking at the resulting play with me.

In the autumn of 1920 Blackburne visited the Liverpool Chess Club and I was lucky enough to play him in a simultaneous. Blackburne was then in his late seventies and impatient clients were complaining that his displays were too slow. I have no regrets at having the following game with him. Naturally he was White.

1	$\frac{\text{P–K4}}{\text{P–K4}}$	2	$\frac{\text{P–KB4}}{\text{B–B4}}$	3	$\frac{\text{Kt–KB3}}{\text{P–Q3}}$	4	$\frac{\text{B–B4}}{\text{Kt–QB3}}$
5	$\frac{\text{P–Q3}}{\text{Kt–B3}}$	6	$\frac{\text{P–B3}}{\text{B–KKt5}}$	7	$\frac{\text{P–KR3}}{\text{B}\times\text{Kt}}$	8	$\frac{\text{Q}\times\text{B}}{\text{Q–K2}}$
9	$\frac{\text{P–B5}}{\text{0–0–0}}$	10	$\frac{\text{B–K3}}{\text{B}\times\text{B}}$	11	$\frac{\text{Q}\times\text{B}}{\text{P–Q4}}$	12	$\frac{\text{B–Kt5}}{\text{P–Q5}}$
13	$\frac{\text{Q–B2}}{\text{R–Q3}}$	14	$\frac{\text{0–0}}{\text{KR–Q1}}$	15	$\frac{\text{B}\times\text{Kt}}{\text{R}\times\text{B}}$	16	$\frac{\text{P–B4}}{\text{Kt–R4}}$
17	$\frac{\text{P–KKt3}}{\text{Q–Kt4}}$	18	$\frac{\text{K–R2}}{\text{Q–K6}}$	19	$\frac{\text{Q–B3}}{\text{R–R3}}$	20	$\frac{\text{Kt–R3}}{}$

Draw agreed.

I was rather proud of the fact that I could not beat England's great veteran chess master, although I had beaten Capablanca a year earlier.

With Blackburne is inevitably linked the name of Amos Burn, not because they had anything in common, but because opinions varied as to who was the greater. Personally, I think Blackburne's wonderful tournament record in the last century provides the answer, but Burn was for many years associated with the Liverpool Chess Club (the Championship Table, with the winners' names on silver plates, bears—or bore, I don't know which—the marks of his hot pipe), and I met many of his supporters. But by the time I met him first, at Edinburgh in 1920, he had retired from tournament chess and somewhat depressed me by telling me that when I reached his age personal glory would count for little.

However, I found him more inspiring at Malvern in 1921 when he insisted on taking me to the 'pictures' to see the film of the Dempsey–Carpentier fight for the Heavyweight Championship of the World.

The first Hastings Congress I took part in was in December 1922 and, during the course of it, I played Richard Reti when he gave a simultaneous blindfold display. The game may well interest admirers of Reti.

	RETI		P–K4		Kt–KB3		P×P
	THOMAS	1	P–QB3	2	P–Q4	3	P×P

	P–Q4		P–B3		P–KR3		B–Q3
4	Kt–QB3	5	B–Kt5	6	B–R4	7	P–K3

	B–KB4		B×B		0–0		QKt–Q2
8	B–Q3	9	Q×B	10	Kt–B3	11	0–0

	R–K1		Q–K2		Q–K3		B×B
12	QR–B1	13	P–QR3	14	B–Kt3	15	RP×B

	Kt–K5		QKt–B3		Kt–Kt5		Q–B4
16	P–QKt4	17	R–B2	18	KR–B1	19	Kt–Q1

	Kt×KtP		Kt×Q		Kt–K2		Kt×P
20	Q×Q	21	P–Kt5	22	P×P	23	R–Kt2

	R–K2		Kt–B3		K–B1		P–R3
24	R–B5	25	P–R4	26	P–R5	27	Kt–Q2

	R–Q1		KR–Q2		Kt–K5		P×Kt
28	Kt–QB3	29	Kt–R4	30	Kt×Kt	31	Kt–Kt6

	R–Q3		R–Q4		R×R		R–Q8 ch.
32	Kt–B4	33	R×P	34	P×R	35	K–R2

	R–Q4		R–R4 ch.		Kt×P		K–Kt1
36	Kt–Kt6	37	K–Kt3	38	R–R7	39	Kt–Q7

40	R–Kt4 ch. K–R3	41	R–R4 ch. K–Kt4	42	R–Kt4 ch. K–B4	43	R×KtP R×RP
44	R×P ch. K–Kt3	45	R–Q7 R–R8 ch.	46	K–R2 Kt–B8 ch.	47	K–Kt1

Drawn.

The first time I played a master in an actual tournament was at the BCF Congress in 1924 at Southport. The great Rubinstein played in the Major Open and scored 100 per cent against his eleven British opponents. My own game was a feeble effort but, here again, admirers of Rubinstein may be interested enough to see it.

THOMAS RUBINSTEIN	1	P–Q4 P–Q4	2	Kt–KB3 Kt–KB3	3	P–B4 P–K3
4	Kt–B3 QKt–Q2	5	B–Kt5 P–B3	6	P–K3 Q–R4	7	Kt–Q2 P×P
8	B×Kt Kt×B	9	Kt×P Q–B2	10	B–Q3 B–K2	11	0–0 0–0
12	R–B1 R–Q1	13	Kt–K5 B–Q2	14	B–Kt1 B–K1	15	Q–B2 QR–B1
16	KR–Q1 P–KKt3	17	Kt–B3 P–B4	18	P×P Q×P	19	R×R R×R
20	R–Q1 R–B1	21	R–Q2 Q–QR4	22	Q–Kt3 P–QKt3	23	P–KR3 K–Kt2
24	K–R2 B–Kt5	25	R–B2 B–Q3 ch.	26	K–Kt1 Kt–Q4	27	Kt×Kt B–R5

Resigns.

A possible continuation could be 28 Q–Q3
B×R 29 Q–Q4 ch.
P–K4

30 Kt×P
Q–K8 ch.

Rubinstein endeared himself to everybody, but he was already showing signs of that mental illness which brought about his withdrawal from world chess.

From 1926 to 1935 I took no part in tournament chess, but after playing at Margate in 1935 I asked Koltanowski to stay with me for a week in 1936 and try to improve my game. This he very kindly did, and told me how his hopes of making a good living as a chess master in Catalonia had been blighted by the Spanish Civil War. A year or two later he came to Blundell's School, Tiverton (where I taught), to give one of his simultaneous blindfold displays before finally finding his chess niche in America.

In 1937 I tied for first place in the Worcester Centenary Congress with Guimard, the Argentine champion, and as a result of this was invited to play in the Hastings Premier Tournament which followed in December.

My first five opponents were Flohr, Reshevsky, Keres, Mikenas and Fine, after which I was let off lightly with Fairhurst, Sir George Thomas, Alexander and Tylor. My net takings were a couple of draws, and my chess was not equal to the company although Reshevsky published our game in his *Best Games of Chess*.

Two memories of that congress stand out. Alekhine had just regained his world title from Euwe and he came to the congress as a spectator. In Holland he had been presented with a cake which showed the final position on the board when he regained his title. Before our first round started, he cut up the cake and gave each of us ten competitors a piece. Every day he watched the play intently and discussed the games afterwards with the players. More and more he convinced me that he truly loved chess and indeed was unable to understand that people could exist who were unable to sacrifice their whole lives to play chess, once they had learnt its beauty. He was an utterly dedicated man.

The other memory is of Keres playing skittles with a fellow compatriot. To my astonishment he gave him the odds of a queen and frequently won. Keres (with Alekhine) had become one of my chess idols, and when I learnt that he produced his own chess magazine, *Eesti Male*, I became a subscriber and still possess the first twenty-four numbers, with the exception of the first which was sold out. When Keres revisited England after the war, I thought he might be interested to know that I possessed these copies, but he laughingly said, 'Oh, they're out of date!'

However, they were not utterly out of date! Another visitor to Hastings after the war was Paul Schmidt who had played a drawn match with Keres in 1936. He told me how sorry he was that in the upheaval of the war he had lost the game-scores of this match and was overjoyed to find that I had No. 3 of *Eesti Male* which gave all seven games. He now has the missing scores.

Three months after my depressing experience at Hastings, I got on a train at London to take me to Margate for the Easter Congress. To my surprise and pleasure I found myself sharing a compartment with Alekhine. He did not refer to Hastings, but told me how much he had enjoyed my win over Guimard in the preceding Worcester Congress. In the first place, I was astonished that he knew of the game at all, and in the second place utterly delighted that he enjoyed it. My morale rose a million. Here is the game:

WORCESTER CENTENARY CONGRESS, 1937

Black: C. E. Guimard

1 P–Q4	Kt–KB3
2 Kt–KB3	P–QKt3
3 P–KKt3	B–Kt2
4 B–Kt2	P–B4
5 0–0	P×P
6 Q×P	P–Kt3
7 Kt–B3	B–Kt2
8 P–K4	Kt–B3
9 Q–R4	....

Deterring P–Q3, and so getting in P–K5 first.

9	0–0
10 P–K5	Kt–K1
11 R–K1	Kt–B2
12 Q–R4	Kt–K3
13 B–R6	Kt–R4
14 Kt–K4	R–B1
15 B–R3	....

White is playing to establish a knight on Kt5 and then to play B×B

15	P–B4

This fails to save the situation. B×Kt would have held things for a time. R–B5 was another possibility.

16 P×P e.p.	P×P
17 B×Kt ch.	P×B
18 B×B	K×B
19 QKt–Kt5	....

My opponent gave a start. He had overlooked this.

19	P×Kt
20 Kt×P	Q–Q7
21 Q×P ch.	K–B3
22 R×P ch.	*Resigns*

C

At the Margate Congress in 1938 I won the following game against Najdorf. Strategically it is interesting in that White won the game on the Q-side and Black demonstrated on the K-side. The usual fashion in the Benoni is the reverse of this.

	THOMAS						
1	$\frac{\text{P–Q4}}{\text{P–QB4}}$	2	$\frac{\text{P–Q5}}{\text{P–K4}}$	3	$\frac{\text{P–K4}}{\text{P–Q3}}$
	NAJDORF						

| 4 | $\frac{\text{B–Q3}}{\text{P–KKt3}}$ | 5 | $\frac{\text{B–K3}}{\text{B–Kt2}}$ | 6 | $\frac{\text{Kt–K2}}{\text{Kt–KR3}}$ | 7 | $\frac{\text{P–KB3}}{\text{P–B4}}$ |

| 8 | $\frac{\text{KKt–B3}}{\text{P–B5}}$ | 9 | $\frac{\text{B–B2}}{\text{P–QR3}}$ | 10 | $\frac{\text{P–QR4}}{\text{P–QKt3}}$ | 11 | $\frac{\text{Kt–R3}}{\text{Kt–Q2}}$ |

| 12 | $\frac{\text{Kt–B4}}{\text{Kt–B2}}$ | 13 | $\frac{\text{R–QKt1}}{\text{R–QKt1}}$ | 14 | $\frac{\text{P–QKt4}}{\text{Q–B2}}$ | 15 | $\frac{\text{0–0}}{\text{B–B3}}$ |

| 16 | $\frac{\text{R–Kt2}}{\text{0–0}}$ | 17 | $\frac{\text{Q–Kt1}}{\text{B–Q1}}$ | 18 | $\frac{\text{Q–R2}}{\text{K–Kt2}}$ | 19 | $\frac{\text{KR–Kt1}}{\text{P–KKt4}}$ |

| 20 | $\frac{\text{P} \times \text{P}}{\text{QP} \times \text{P}}$ | 21 | $\frac{\text{R–Kt3}}{\text{Kt–Q3}}$ | 22 | $\frac{\text{Q–Kt2}}{\text{Kt} \times \text{Kt}}$ | 23 | $\frac{\text{B} \times \text{Kt}}{\text{Q–Q3}}$ |

To make any headway in this position White must transfer his knight from QB3 to QB4. I managed to discover this, although making five moves with the knight, instead of three.

| 24 | $\frac{\text{Kt–K2}}{\text{B–B3}}$ | 25 | $\frac{\text{Kt–B1}}{\text{B–Kt2}}$ | 26 | $\frac{\text{Q–B3}}{\text{KR–B1}}$ | 27 | $\frac{\text{Kt–Q3}}{\text{B–Q1}}$ |

| 28 | $\frac{\text{Kt–Kt2}}{\text{Q–KB3}}$ | 29 | $\frac{\text{B–B1}}{\text{R–R1}}$ | 30 | $\frac{\text{Kt–B4}}{\text{KR–Kt1}}$ | 31 | $\frac{\text{Q–Kt2}}{\text{B–B2}}$ |

| 32 | $\frac{\text{B–K1}}{\text{P–Kt4}}$ | 33 | $\frac{\text{P} \times \text{P}}{\text{P} \times \text{P}}$ | 34 | $\frac{\text{R} \times \text{P}}{\text{B–R3}}$ | 35 | $\frac{\text{R} \times \text{R}}{\text{R} \times \text{R}}$ |

| 36 | $\frac{\text{Q–R2}}{\text{B} \times \text{Kt}}$ | 37 | $\frac{\text{B} \times \text{B}}{\text{R} \times \text{R}}$ | 38 | $\frac{\text{Q} \times \text{R}}{\text{Q–QKt3}}$ | 39 | $\frac{\text{Q} \times \text{Q}}{\text{Kt} \times \text{Q}}$ |

| 40 | $\frac{\text{B–Kt5}}{\text{Kt–B1}}$ | 41 | $\frac{\text{B–R6}}{\text{Kt–Q3}}$ | 42 | $\frac{\text{K–B2}}{\text{P–R4}}$ | 43 | $\frac{\text{P–R3}}{\text{P–R5}}$ |

44 $\dfrac{\text{B–B3}}{\text{K–B3}}$ 45 $\dfrac{\text{K–K1}}{\text{Kt–K1}}$ 46 $\dfrac{\text{K–K2}}{\text{Kt–Q3}}$ 47 $\dfrac{\text{K–Q2}}{\text{K–K2}}$

48 $\dfrac{\text{K–B1}}{\text{Kt–K1}}$ 49 $\dfrac{\text{K–Kt2}}{\text{K–Q3}}$ 50 $\dfrac{\text{K–Kt3}}{\text{Kt–B3}}$ 51 $\dfrac{\text{B–Kt5}}{\text{B–Kt3}}$

52 $\dfrac{\text{B–K1}}{\text{Kt–R4}}$ 53 $\dfrac{\text{K–R4}}{\text{Kt–Kt6}}$ 54 $\dfrac{\text{B–B4}}{\text{Kt–R8}}$ 55 $\dfrac{\text{K–Kt5}}{\text{B–Q1}}$

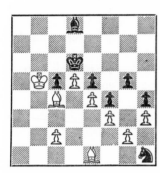

The main point of this endgame is that when White attacks the QBP with his bishop on QR3, Black cannot defend with his bishop on QR2 because of $\dfrac{\text{K–R6}}{\text{B–Kt1}}$ $\dfrac{\text{K–Kt7}}{\text{B–B2}}$ B × P ch.

Accordingly Black sacrifices a pawn on the K side in order to be able to defend from KB7. But in the process he gets in Zugzwang.

56 $\dfrac{\text{B–B3}}{\text{Kt–B7}}$ 57 $\dfrac{\text{B–K2}}{\text{P–Kt5}}$ 58 $\dfrac{\text{RP × P}}{\text{P–R6}}$ 59 $\dfrac{\text{P × P}}{\text{Kt × RP}}$

60 $\dfrac{\text{B–Kt2}}{\text{B–R5}}$ 61 $\dfrac{\text{B–B3}}{\text{B–Q1}}$ 62 $\dfrac{\text{B–K1}}{\text{Kt–Kt8}}$ 63 $\dfrac{\text{B–Q1}}{\text{Kt–R6}}$

64 $\dfrac{\text{K–B4}}{}$ Zugzwang. The black B must stay on Q1 to prevent the white one entering at QR5 or KR4. 64 $\dfrac{}{\text{Kt–Kt4}}$ 65 $\dfrac{\text{B–B2}}{\textit{Resigns}}$

Before the war came I had formed a friendship with Lodewijk Prins whose piano-playing I greatly admired. After the war it was through him that I received an invitation to play in a chess congress at Maastricht and, while there, we decided to go by train to Liège to visit the birthplace of César Franck. As the train approached the city, I asked Prins how we would find the birthplace in a city of 150,000 people. 'Ask the first person we meet,' he replied. 'But surely he will be unlikely to know,' I objected. 'Of course he will know.' And it was so.

To get to Maastricht from Amsterdam, Prins and I were very kindly driven through war-devastated Holland by Dr M. Euwe. Not only was there much devastation, but there was the memory for Dutchmen of the last winter of the war, 'Starvation Winter', when food was nearly non-existent. It was understandable, therefore, that Dr Euwe, in common with many other chess masters, was very bitter over Alekhine's alleged collaboration with the Nazis in writing anti-Semitic chess articles.

Alexander played at Maastricht and two memories remain. He had recently been awarded the CBE and a Dutch friend enquired, 'Does this mean you are a knight?' 'Alas, barely a tempo,' was his modest reply.

At the opening of the congress the burgomeister gave his address in three languages. 'How many English mayors could do that?' was Alexander's query.

Two years later I had the chance to play Dr Euwe again in a tournament. (I had previously lost to him at Bournemouth in 1939.)

PLYMOUTH JUBILEE CONGRESS, 1948

Black: Dr M. Euwe

1 P–K4	P–K4
2 P–KB4	P×P
3 Kt–KB3	B–K2
4 B–B4	Kt–KB3
5 P–K5	Kt–Kt5
6 0–0	....

6 P–Q4 was preferred a year later since the reply ...., P–Q4 is suspect owing to 7 P×P e.p., B×P; 8 Q–K2 ch., Q–K2; 9 Q×Q ch., K×Q; 10 Kt–B3 with advantage (Horne–Barden, Hastings).

6	Kt–QB3
7 P–Q4	P–Q4
8 P×P e.p.	B×P
9 R–K1 ch.	Kt–K2

Here the position is given as equal in *Modern Chess Openings.*

10 P–KR3	Kt–B3
11 Kt–K5	B×Kt
12 P×B	Q×Q
13 R×Q	Kt–R4
14 Kt–B3	B–B4
15 B–K2	Kt–Kt6

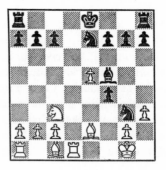

16 B–Kt5 ch. . . . .

The only move to keep equality.

16 . . . .   P–B3
17 B × KBP   Kt–K5

Kt–R4; 18 B–Kt5, P × B; 19 Kt × P is in White's favour.

18 Kt × Kt   B × Kt
19 B–Q3   B × B
20 R × B   Kt–Kt3
21 B–Kt3   R–Q1

A complex situation has resolved into an endgame in which White's isolated pawn is a weakness.

22 QR–Q1   K–K2
23 K–B2   R × R
24 R × R   R–Q1
25 R × R   K × R
26 K–K3   K–K2
27 K–K4   K–K3
28 P–B4   . . . .

28 . . . .   P–KR4

Immediately after the game, Euwe pointed out that P–KR3 would have threatened 29. . . ., Kt × P. Thus 30 B × Kt, P–B4 ch.; 31 K–Q4, P–B4 ch. (or K–B4, P–Kt4 ch.). This pretty combination was new to me, but is one to remember.

29 P–Kt3   P–Kt3
30 P–QR4   P–B4

White has only one way to avoid Zugzwang.

31 P–R5   P × P

Black too has little option

32 B–B2   Kt × P
33 B × P   P–B4 ch.
34 K–K3   P–QR5

34 . . . ., Kt–B3; 35 K–B4 favours White!

35 P × P   Kt × P ch.
36 K–Q4   Kt–K4
37 B–B8   P–Kt3
38 B–Kt7   Kt–Q2
39 K–B4   K–Q3
40 K–Kt5   K–B2
41 P–R5   P–Kt4
42 B–Q4   P–B5

Draw agreed

In December 1950, thirteen years later, I was back in the Hastings Premier Tournament, and partly redeemed the earlier effort by scoring 50 per cent. My chief recollection of this congress is about Weaver Adams, whose original views on opening theory were well known in the USA, as he had published them there in his book, *Simple Chess*. He had grown tired of meeting opponents in the USA who had studied his opening theory and he was looking forward to springing surprises on his English opponents. However, he did not meet with the success he anticipated, and his consternation at the end of the tournament, when he found out that Leonard Barden had not only studied *Simple Chess* but had also passed it around, was really quite comical, although one could not help sympathising with him a little.

My own game with him owed not a little to a study of his book.

HASTINGS CHRISTMAS CONGRESS, 1950–1

White: Weaver W. Adams

1 P–K4	P–K4	19 QR–KKt1	K–K2
2 Kt–QB3	Kt–KB3	20 K–B1	B–Q2
3 B–B4	Kt–B3	21 K–K1	QR–R1
4 P–Q3	B–Kt5	22 K–Q2	QR–R2
5 B–KKt5	P–KR3	23 K–B1	Q–Kt2
6 B×Kt	B×Kt ch.	24 B–B1	Q–R1
7 P×B	Q×B	25 B–Kt2	....
8 Kt–K2	Kt–K2		
9 0–0	P–KKt4		
10 Kt–Kt3	....		

So far all as in *Simple Chess* under the heading 'White to Play and Win'.

10 ....   P–KR4

I had decided that this was an improvement on the variation in his book: 10 ...., Kt–Kt3; 11 Kt–R5, Q–K2; 12 P–Kt3, P–Q3; 13 K–R1.

11 Kt×P	Q–R3
12 P–Kt4	Kt–Kt3
13 Q–B3	Kt–B5
14 P–KR3	P–Q3
15 P–Q4	P–KB3
16 Kt×Kt	KtP×Kt
17 K–Kt2	Q–Kt4
18 R–R1	R–R5

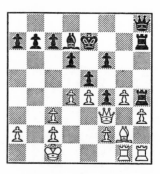

White has successfully defended his K wing. Can he hold his Q wing also?

25 ....   B–Kt4
26 Q–Q1   ....

He would have had much more freedom if he had given back his pawn with P–B4.

26 ....   B–B5

27 K–Kt2	Q–K1
28 K–R1	....

The end of a long walk.

28	Q–R5
29 Q–Kt1	Q–R4
30 Q–Kt2	P–B6

The breakthrough.

31 B×P	R×P
32 P–R3	R×R
33 B×R	....

33 R×R, R×R; 34 B×R, P×P; 35 P×P, Q–K8 ch.; 36 Q–Kt1, Q–B6 ch.; 37 Q–Kt2, Q–R6; 38 Q–B1, B–B8; 39 B–B3, Q×B; 40 Q×B, Q×P ch.; 41 K–Kt1, Q–Kt5 ch. followed by Q×P was also good for Black.

33	R–R6
34 P–B3	B–K7

Here the game was adjourned, but White resigned without playing on. His sealed move was Q–Kt4 and the game could have continued Q×Q; 36 RP×Q, K–B2.

Tartakower came frequently to the Southsea Chess Congress and stayed at the same boarding-house each year where, in the intervals between playing chess, he resumed copying out the *Encyclopaedia Britannica* from where he had left off the preceding year. He was a cheerful soul whose usual salutation was 'Bravo!' The two following games, but with very abbreviated notes, are taken from *100 Master Games of Modern Chess* which he wrote in collaboration with du Mont. His annotations of his loss to me are typically generous.

HASTINGS CHRISTMAS CONGRESS, 1950–1

Black: W. Unzicker

1 PK–4	P–K4
2 Kt–KB3	Kt–QB3
3 B–B4	B–B4
4 P–QKt4	B×P
5 P–B3	B–R4
6 P–Q4	P–Q3
7 Q–Kt3	Kt×P

An obviously risky line in which, at the cost of losing the option of castling, Black relies on maintaining his extra pawn. But Black cannot play Q–K2 on account of 8 P–Q5, Kt–Q5; 9 Kt×Kt, P×Kt; 10 Q–R4 ch. followed by Q×B. In order to avoid this, Black at this point usually plays Q–Q2 after which White still has some awkward threats, as shown in the game from a qualifying tournament in the World Junior Championship, 1951; Malcolm Barker–W. Marshall. 8 P×P, B–Kt3; 9 QKt–Q2, Kt–R4; 10 Q–B2, Kt–K2; 11 B×P ch., K×B; 12 P–K6 ch., K×P; 13 Kt–Kt5

ch., K–B3; 14 P–K5 ch. P×P;
15 QKt–K4 ch., K–Kt3; 16
Kt–B3, QKt–B3 (or 16 . . . .,
Q–Q4; 17 P–B4, Kt×P; 18
Kt–B3 dis. ch., B–B4; 19
Kt–R4 ch.); 17 Kt–B5 dis. ch.,
Q–B4; 18 Kt–R4 ch., *Resigns*

8 Kt×Kt   P×Kt
9 B×P ch.   K–B1
10 0–0   Q–K2

The immediate development
by Kt–B3 would be bad
because of P–K5.

11 B–QB4   Kt–B3
12 P×P   Kt×P
13 Q–B3 ch. Kt–B3
14 Kt–B3   B×Kt

On the well-tried principle
that, in a difficult defensive
position, exchanges are to be
recommended. If, instead, P–B3,
White plays 15 B–R3 followed
by by QR–K1, and Black's
position is most precarious.

15 Q×B   B–B4
16 R–K1   Q–Q2
17 B–KKt5   Kt–K5

If R–K1, there follows 18
B×Kt, R×R ch.; 19 R×R,
P×B; 20 Q–B3, P–B3; 21
B–K6, B×B; 22 Q×P ch. with
a quick win for White.

18 R×Kt   B×R
19 R–K1   P–Q4

Appears to save the situation,
but is refuted by White's brilliant
rejoinder. On the whole Q–Kt5
provides the most promising
defence, although 20 P–B3,
Q×B; 21 P×B or 20 B–KB1,

Q×B; 21 R×B would have set
Black some difficult problems.

20 R×B   . . . .

A second sacrifice of the
exchange, and one of great
beauty. With the black king
unfavourably placed, the two
mobile bishops are superior to
the disconnected rooks.

20 . . . .   P×R

Compulsory, for if P×B;
21 Q–B3 ch. wins at once.

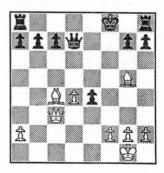

21 Q–KKt3   . . . .

A pity! He misses a win in
the grand manner by 21 Q–Kt4
ch., Q–Q3; 22 Q×P, R–K1;
23 B–Q2, Q–Q1; 24 B–Kt4 ch.,
R–K2; 25 Q×KP, P–Kt3; 26
Q–K6, K–K1; 27 B–Kt5 ch.,
K–B1; 28 Q–B6 ch., K–Kt1;
29 B–B4 ch., with mate to
follow.

21 . . . .   Q–Q3
22 Q–Kt4   P–KKt3

The magical saving clause.

23 B–R6 ch.   K–K1
24 Q×KP ch.   K–Q2
25 Q–Kt4 ch. K–K1

26 Q–K4 ch.	K–Q2
27 Q–Kt4 ch.	K–K1
Draw	

A most creditable performance by White against the winner of the tournament.

SOUTHSEA CONGRESS, 1951

White: Dr S. Tartakower

Notes abbreviated from *100 Master Games of Modern Chess* by Tartakower and du Mont.

The following game is a magnificent illustration of the theme, 'How to take advantage of your opponent's mistakes'.

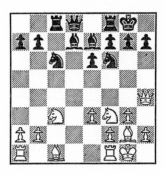

1 Kt–KB3	P–Q4
2 P–KKt3	Kt–KB3
3 B–Kt2	P–K3
4 0–0	P–B4
5 P–Q4	Kt–B3
6 P–B4	QP×P
7 Q–R4	....

Another sound plan is Kt–K5 (Keres–Klein, 1946).

7	B–Q2
8 P×P	B×P

Another idea is 8 ...., Kt–QR4; 9 Q–B2, B×P; 10 Kt–K5, P–KR3.

9 Q×BP	B–K2

A reasoned retreat. Neither Q–Kt3 nor Q–K2 is satisfactory.

10 Kt–B3	R–QB1
11 Q–KR4	....

Risky and not yet necessary.

11	0–0

12 P–K4	....

White underestimates the danger to his queen which, after this move and Black's reply, is cut off from the centre and the Q side. Playable, rather, is R–Q1.

12	P–K4

Bravo! At a stroke White's position has become tragic.

13 B–R3	....

This loses ingloriously. He should, in any event, try R–Q1 or B–Kt5.

13	Kt–Q5

Excellent judgment. White expected Kt–KKt5 when the Q

escapes after 14 Kt–KKt5, P–KR3; 15 B×Kt, P×Kt; 16 Q–R3.

14 Kt×P   ....

If Kt×Kt, Black wins an important pawn after ...., P×Kt; 15 Kt–K2, B×B; 16 Q×B, Kt×P.

14 ....   Kt–Kt5

The death sentence for the white queen.

15 B×Kt   B×Q
16 Kt×B   P–B4

17 Kt×R   P×B
18 B–K3   ....

If 18 P×B, Q×P; 19 B–B4, R×QKt; 20 B–Kt3, R×B ch.; 21 BP×R, Kt–K7 ch.; 22 K–B2, Q×RP ch.

18 ....   Kt–B6 ch.
19 K–R1   Q×Kt
20 P×B   Q–Q3

Resigns

Black has taken advantage of his opportunity in a masterly manner.

5 The Sicilian Defence

The main variations of this opening are so well known that the side-lines are well worth exploring.

It has always been held that the Wing Gambit is unsound, but Frank Marshall wrote in *My Fifty Years of Chess*, 'This gambit leads to some beautiful combinations and positions. Like all gambits, the idea is to secure a strong centre, quick development and a chance for combinations.'

He followed these words up with some analysis, so I decided to try the Wing Gambit.

After some early successes (see the games against T. H. Tylor and L. 'Smith') I had such utter failure at Hastings 1951–2 in my games against Gligoric and Lothar Schmid that I abandoned the gambit for twelve years. However, in 1963 it came to life again (see the games against Hollis and Hindle), and it can be recommended as an occasional weapon to the player who wants a sharp game.

The other variation which I have adopted is 2 P–QB3. I was attracted to this when I found from *Alekhine's Best Games of Chess 1938–45* that the World Champion himself was experimenting with this move in his last period. The notes which Alexander gives are valuable.

Black generally chooses between 2 P–Q4 and 2 Kt–KB3 which lead to different types of game. I have given three examples of each which will, I hope, show some of the possibilities to be looked for.

Finally, I have added a correspondence game in which the main variation took a most unexpected turn.

SEMI-FINAL COUNTIES CHAMPIONSHIP, 1951

DEVON *v.* OXFORDSHIRE

Black: T. H. Tylor

1 P–K4	P–QB4
2 P–QKt4	P×P
3 Kt–KB3	P–Q4
4 P×P	Q×P

Black does better to play Kt–KB3, when White should reply P–QR3.

5 P–Q4	B–Kt5
6 B–K2	Kt–QB3

This move, played before P–K3, sets one thinking in terms of P–Q5.

7 0–0	....

And so 7 P–B4, P×P e.p.; 8 Kt×P, Q–QR4 would be sharper.

7	R–Q1

Continuing the pressure on the QP at the expense of K-side development.

8 B–Kt2	P–K3
9 P–B4	P×P e.p.
10 Kt×P	Q–QR4
11 Q–Kt3	KKt–K2
12 KR–K1	B×Kt
13 B×B	Kt×P
14 Q×P	Q–Kt3

15 QR–Kt1	....

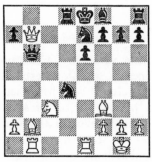

Black refrains from playing Q×Q as the white KB would remain a powerful attacking piece. He should, however, have played KKt–B3 when I should have had to struggle to draw.

15	Kt×B ch.
16 Q×Kt	Q–B3
17 Kt–K4	....

White has now a fine position and his attack should succeed.

17	Kt–Q4
18 QR–Q1	P–KR3
19 Kt–B3	B–K2

Black has no good move.

20 Kt×Kt	P×Kt
21 B×P	KR–Kt1
22 B–B6	R–Q2
23 R–QB1	Q–R3

Attempting to ward off both R–B8 and Q–R3.

24 B×B	R×B
25 R×R ch.	K×R

| 26 R–B7 ch. | K–Q1 | Mate is inevitable after Q–Q3, |
| 27 Q × BP | *Resigns* | 28 R × P. |

HASTINGS CHRISTMAS CONGRESS, 1950–1

Black: L. 'Smith' (the *nom-de-guerre* for this congress of one of Holland's strongest players)

1 P–K4	P–QB4
2 P–QKt4	P × P
3 P–Q4	Kt–KB3
4 P–K5	Kt–Q4
5 B–QB4	Kt–Kt3
6 B–Kt3	P–Q4
7 P × P e.p.	Q × P
8 Kt–KB3	B–B4
9 0–0	P–K3
10 P–B4	P × P e.p.
11 Kt × P	B–K2

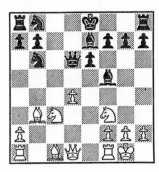

12 P–Q5 . . . .

The start of a succession of threats, the first of which is Kt–QKt5 followed by P–Q6.

| 12 . . . . | P × P |
| 13 B × P | . . . . |

Here the White Kt is a more powerful attacking weapon than the B.

| 13 . . . . | Kt × B |

The alternative Kt–B3; 14 Kt–QKt5, Q–Q2; 15 B × Kt, Q × B; 16 KKt–Q4, is not attractive.

| 14 Kt × Kt | . . . . |

Now the threat is B–B4 followed by Kt–B7.

14	B–K3
15 Q–R4 ch.	Kt–Q2
16 Kt × B	Q × Kt
17 B–R3	. . . .

White's attack has got through. Now for the kill!

17	Q–B3
18 KR–K1	P–QR3
19 Kt–K5	R–Q1
20 Kt–B4	R–QKt1
21 Kt–Kt6	K–Q1
22 QR–Q1	Q–B4
23 R × B	*Resigns*

WEST OF ENGLAND CHAMPIONSHIP, 1963

Black: A. S. Hollis

| 1 P–K4 | P–QB4 | 3 P–QR3 | P–K3 |
| 2 P–QKt4 | P × P | 4 P × P | B × P |

5 P–QB3	B–B1
6 P–Q4	P–Q4
7 P–K5	Kt–QB3

The opening has now some of the characteristics of a French Defence.

8 Kt–B3	P–B4
9 P×P e.p.	Kt×P
10 B–Q3	B–Q3
11 0–0	0–0
12 R–K1	B–Q2
13 Kt–K5	Q–B2
14 B–R3	Kt×Kt
15 B×B	Kt–B6 ch.
16 Q×Kt	Q×B
17 R–K5	....

White has still a little pressure, but his Q side is undeveloped, and he has not enough compensation for his P.

17	P–QR3
18 Q–R3	Q–Kt3
19 R–R2	Q–Kt6
20 QR–K2	Kt–K5

Black threatens mate. I hoped he would keep up this threat after my next move.

| 21 B–B2 | Q–Kt7 |

He does so! (Threatening mate, the win of White's B and keeping the White Kt firmly anchored at QKt1.)

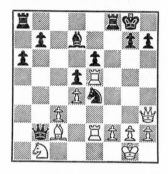

22 Q×P ch. ....

The saving move, and not very difficult to discover.

22 ....   K×Q

Black is a little shaken, otherwise he would have opted for K–B2.

23 B×Kt ch.	P×B
24 R×Q	P–QKt4
25 Kt–Q2	QR–B1
26 Kt×P	R–QB5

27 P–B3 and White won on Move 58.

COUNTIES CHAMPIONSHIP, 1963

DEVON *v.* WARWICKSHIRE

Black: O. M. Hindle

| 1 P–K4 | P–QB4 |
| 2 P–QKt4 | P–QKt3 |

Reasonable enough, although not to be recommended.

| 3 P×P | P×P |
| 4 Kt–KB3 | B–Kt2 |

| 5 Kt–B3 | P–K3 |
| 6 QR–Kt1 | Q–B2 |

Black's Q is unhappily placed here. His opening strategy has been weak.

| 7 P–Q4 | P×P |

8 Kt–QKt5	Q–B3
9 B–Q3	Kt–B3
10 KKt×P	Q–B1
11 B–KB4	Kt–R3
12 0–0	B–B4
13 Q–K2	....

13 ....   P–Q4

Black is at a loss for a good move. The natural 0–0 would be followed by 14 Kt–Q6, B×Kt; 15 B×B threatening both B×R and R×B.

14 Kt–Q6 ch.	B×Kt
15 B×B	P×P

Kt×P cannot be played because of B×Kt and Q–Kt5 ch.

16 R×B	Q×R

P×B was about equally bad.

17 B×Kt	Q–Q4
18 Kt–Kt5	K–Q2
19 R–Q1	Q–B3
20 Kt–B7	QR–Kt1
21 B–Kt5	R×B
22 Q×R	Q×Q
23 Kt×Q	K–B3

Instead of this, I had expected resignation. But I was short of time and Black has hopes of regaining a piece with R–Q1.

24 Kt–B3	Kt–Q4
25 Kt×P	P–B4
26 Kt–Kt5	P–KR3
27 Kt–B7	R–QB1
28 B–R3	Kt–B6
29 R–Q3	Kt×P
30 P–QB4	K–Kt3
31 P–B5 ch.	and Black

resigned on his 40th move.

BRITISH CHAMPIONSHIP, 1956

Black: M. F. Collins

1 P–K4	P–QB4
2 P–QB3	P–Q4
3 P×P	Q×P
4 P–Q4	Kt–QB3
5 Kt–B3	B–Kt5
6 B–K2	P×P
7 P×P	P–K3

So far all as in Alekhine–Podgorny, Prague 1942. For notes on the variation see *Alekhine's Best Games 1938–45*.

8 0–0	Kt–B3

The Alekhine game continued 8 Kt–B3, B–Kt5; 9 0–0 Q–QR4; 10 P–QR3, Kt–B3?; 11 P–Q5, P×P; 12 P×B, Q×R; 13 Kt–Q2.

9 Kt–B3	Q–Q1

He probably disliked Q–QR4, 10 B–Q2.

10 Q–R4   R–B1

To meet the threatened Kt–K5.

11 B–KKt5   . . . .

With the threat of B×Kt followed by P–Q5.

11 . . . .   B–R4

To counter the threat

12 P–Q5   . . . .

The thematic move. White has a winning attack.

12 . . . .   P×P

13 QR–Q1   . . . .

Black's QB will again be in trouble after the threatened R×P.

13 . . . .   Q–R4
14 Q×Q   Kt×Q
15 B×Kt   P×B
16 B–Kt5 ch. Kt–B3
17 KR–K1 ch. B–K2
18 Kt×P   B×Kt
19 P×B   K–B1
20 B×Kt   *Resigns*

WARD-HIGGS CORRESPONDENCE

DEVON *v*. LEICESTERSHIRE, 1961–2

Black: V. H. Woodward

1 P–K4	P–QB4
2 P–QB3	P–Q4
3 P×P	Q×P
4 P–Q4	P–K3
5 Kt–KB3	Kt–QB3
6 B–K2	Kt–B3
7 0–0	P×P
8 P×P	B–K2
9 Kt–B3	Q–QR4
10 B–KB4	0–0
11 P–QR3	Kt–Q4
12 Kt×Kt	P×Kt

Appears to free the QB,

but now Black also has an isolated pawn. The game would have taken a different course after Q×Kt, 13 R–B1.

13 P–QKt4	Q–Kt3
14 P–Kt5	Kt–Q1

Black would be in trouble after Kt–R4; 15 Q–R4.

15 Q–Kt3	Kt–K3
16 B–K3	R–Q1
17 B–Q3	B–B3
18 KR–Q1	Q–Q3
19 Q–Kt4	Q–Kt1

Were Black to exchange queens, his Q side would be very weak.

20 P–Kt3	P–KKt3
21 QR–B1	B–Q2
22 P–KR4	R–QB1
23 R × R ch.	B × R

Black is playing to restrain Kt–K5–Kt4.

24 R–QB1	B–Q2
25 Kt–K5	....

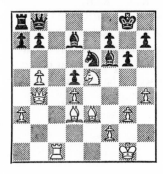

The assault begins. It is difficult to believe that Black will resign after playing 9 more moves. Apart from attacking the bishop, White threatens Kt–Kt4.

25	B × Kt
26 P × B	Q × P

Otherwise White plays Q–Q6.

27 Q–K7	B–K1
28 Q × KtP	R–Q1
29 Q–K7	....

Much stronger than capturing the RP.

29	P–Q5

I had intended to answer Q–Kt7 with P–R5.

30 B–Kt5	B × P

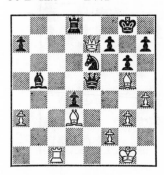

If Black cannot play this, he is lost. But this also loses.

31 B–B6	Q–Q4
32 B × B	Q × B
33 Q × R ch.	Kt × Q
34 R–B8	*Resigns*

BRITISH CHAMPIONSHIP, 1961

Black: B. H. Wood

1 P–K4	P–QB4
2 P–QB3	P–Q4
3 P × P	Q × P
4 P–Q4	P–K4
5 P × KP	....

It may be that Kt–KB3 is best in this sharp variation.

5	Q × Q ch.
6 K × Q	Kt–QB3
7 Kt–B3	....

Now I thought Black would have to decide between B–Kt5

D

and B–B4 (with its obvious restrictions for White).

8 . . . .   B–Kt5

So the pawn is to be regained. I was rather glad.

8 B–KB4   KKt–K2
9 K–B2   Kt–Kt3
10 B–Kt3   B×Kt
11 P×B   KKt×P
12 Kt–R3   B–K2
13 R–K1   . . . .

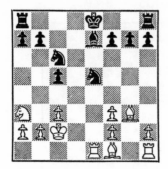

13 . . . .   Kt×P

Too greedy. He should have played Kt–Kt3 with an approximately level position.

14 R–K3   Kt–Kt4
15 P–KB4   Kt–K3
16 P–B5   KKt–Q1
17 B–Q6   K–Q2
18 B×B   Kt×B
19 B–R3   P–B3
20 R–Q1 ch.   K–K1
21 Kt–Kt5 K–B1
22 R–Q7   Kt(K2)–B3
23 Kt–B7   *Resigns*

Black should have preferred 22 . . . . Kt(Q1)–B3; but his game would have been dismal after 23 R×P.

HASTINGS CHALLENGERS, 1964–5

Black: M. J. Basman

1 P–K4   P–QB4
2 P–QB3   Kt–KB3
3 P–K5   Kt–Q4
4 P–Q4   P×P
5 P×P   . . . .

5 Q×P has been experimented with recently. After P–K3; 6 B–QB4, Kt–QB3; 7 Q–K4 Black should not play P–B4; 8 Q–K2 but rather P–Q3; 8 P×P, Kt–B3; followed by 0–0.

For 5 B–QB4 see the next game.

5 . . . .   P–Q3
6 Kt–KB3   Kt–QB3
7 Kt–B3   Kt×Kt

Wrong. Black should play P×P. My game with Dr J. Penrose in the British Championship, 1960, continued 7 . . . . P×P; 8 P×P, Kt×Kt; 9 Q×Q ch., Kt×Q; 10 P×Kt, P–K3; 11 B–Kt5 ch., B–Q2; 12 B×B ch., K×B; 13 B–K3, K–B2; 14 P–QR4, Kt–B3; 15 K–K2, B–K2; 16 KR–QKt1, KR–Q1; 17 R–Kt5, QR–B1; 18 QR–

QKt1 ?(P–R5!), P–QKt3.
Black had the better game.

8 P×Kt   P×P

After this Black's game was
very difficult.

9 P–Q5   P–K5

The only alternative would
be Kt–Kt1.

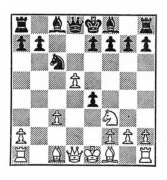

10 P×Kt   Q×Q ch.
11 K×Q   P×Kt
12 B–QKt5   K–Q1

P–QKt3 followed by P–QR3
was better for Black than this.

13 B–KB4   B–Kt5

No time for BP×P; 14 P–B7
mate. Or KtP×P; 14 B×P,
B–Kt5; 15 K–B2.

14 K–B2   B–B4 ch.

To P×P White replies 15
KR–Q1 ch., B×R; 16 R×B
ch., K–B1; 17 P–B7

15 K–Kt2   K–B1
16 KR–Q1   P–Kt4
17 R–Q8 ch. *Resigns*

ENGLAND *v.* CZECHOSLOVAKIA, CORRESPONDENCE, 1965–6

Black: F. Cvachoucek

1 P–K4	P–QB4
2 P–QB3	Kt–KB3
3 P–K5	Kt–Q4
4 P–Q4	P×P
5 B–QB4	....

A version of the Morra
Gambit.

5 ....   Kt–Kt3

Black can also play Q–B2;
6 Q–K2, P–Q6; 7 B×P (or
Q–K4), Kt–Kt5?!, or Q–B2;
6 Q–K2, Kt–Kt3; 7 B–Kt3,
P–Q6; 8 Q–K4.

6 B–Kt3   P–Q3

For P×P see the next game.

7 Kt–KB3   P–K3

8 BP×P	Kt–B3
9 B–Kt5	B–K2
10 B×B	Q×B
11 P×P	Q×P
12 Kt–B3	0–0
13 0–0	P–QR3

An unnecessary precaution.
Black should be thinking how
to develop his Q side.

14 Kt–K4	Q–K2
15 Q–K2	P–K4

Develops his QB apparently,
but the White QP has other
ideas!

16 P–Q5	Kt–R4
17 P–Q6	Q–K1

18 Kt–B5	Kt × B
19 P × Kt	P–B3
20 KR–Q1	Q–B2
21 Kt–Q2	R–Q1
22 Kt(Q2)–K4	R–Kt1

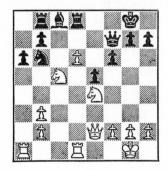

HASTINGS CHRISTMAS CONGRESS, 1959–60

Black: A. Zehnder

In spite of its disastrous finish, this game has its amusing side.

1 P–K4	P–QB4
2 P–QB3	Kt–KB3
3 P–K5	Kt–Q4
4 P–Q4	P × P
5 B–QB4	Kt–Kt3
6 B–Kt3	P × P
7 Kt × P	Kt–B3
8 Kt–B3	P–Q3
9 0–0	P–K3

Better than P × P; 10 Kt × P, P–K3; 11 Q × Q ch., Kt × Q; 12 Kt–Kt5.

10 B–Kt5	B–K2
11 B × B	Kt × B
12 P × P	Kt–B4
13 Kt–K4	B–Q2
14 Kt–K5	0–0

23 P–Q7	. . . .

This pawn's lust to expand is decisive.

23	B × P

Clearly not Kt × P; 24 Kt–Q6 followed by Q–B4 ch.

24 Kt × KtP!	R × Kt

Or R–KB1; 25 R × P.

25 Kt–Q6	*Resigns*

15 Q–R5	P–Kt3
16 Q–R3	B–B3
17 Kt × B	P × Kt
18 KR–Q1	Kt–Q4
19 P–Q7	. . . .

Another pawn with a lust to expand. It is quite safe.

19	Q–K2
20 QR–B1	Kt–Q3

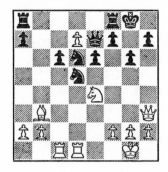

Onlookers found this position amusing, and wanted to know whether my P on Q7 was really a Black pawn which had lost some of its paint.

21 Kt–B5	QR–Kt1
22 R–K1	R–Kt5
23 R×P	....

The wrong piece. Kt×P was much better.

23	P×R
24 Q×P ch.	R–B2??

Disastrous. Q–B2 would have defended his Kt on Q3 with a mating threat. Q×Q would also have probably drawn.

25 Q×Q	*Resigns*

WARD–HIGGS CORRESPONDENCE

DEVON *v.* NORFOLK, 1956

Black: A. Spiller

1 P–K4	P–QB4
2 Kt–KB3	P–Q3
3 P–Q4	P×P
4 Kt×P	Kt–KB3
5 Kt–QB3	P–QR3
6 B–KKt5	QKt–Q2
7 Q–Q2	P–Kt4

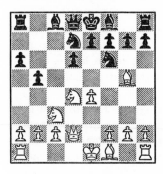

8 P–QR4	....

Initiating a very sharp line.

8	P–Kt5
9 Kt–Q5	Kt×P
10 Q×P	....

Threatening Kt–B6.

10	R–QKt1
11 Kt–Kt5	P×Kt

If R×Kt; 12 P×R, Kt×B; 13 P×P wins.

12 Q×Kt	P×P
13 Q×P	P–R3
14 Q–B6	*Resigns*

R–Kt2 is answered by R–R8, P–B4 by B–QB4, and P–B3 by Kt–B7 ch. followed by Q–Q5 ch.

6 A Few Scalps

Since schooldays it has been my habit to keep a record of all match or tournament games. Some ten years or so ago I decided to go through this collection and sort out the 'Best Games'. This reduced the collection to about ninety. In the course of time some of these became jettisoned, but the collection still stood at around seventy. Now, when the time has come to see if any are indeed worth publication, there has been another vast consignment to limbo. Whether, in fact, the specimens left in this chapter (four out of over 200 games played in the British Championship, five from a similar number played at Hastings, and four others [one a correspondence game]) are worth preservation is somewhat dubious. Probably, were my play to improve, I should want to jettison the lot. But I am buoyed up by the belief that they will be found of interest by the majority of British chess players, if not by the small group at the very top.

In addition to these thirteen games, there are five game positions. One is from my loss to R. F. Combe when he won the British Championship in 1946. I should like to record here what a great player I thought he was, and how sorry I was that he died prematurely. Another thing worth recording about him is that he played very quickly in 1946, and frequently had a whole hour to spare on his clock.

Another game-position is my 'swindle' against J. Penrose in 1949 which may encourage a few hopefuls by showing that the greatest have moments of error. It is worth adding that Penrose made an equal fool of me at Aberystwyth in 1961, when he caught me in what was then a little-known trap:

PENROSE				
THOMAS	1 $\frac{\text{P–K4}}{\text{P–K4}}$	2 $\frac{\text{Kt–KB3}}{\text{Kt–QB3}}$	3 $\frac{\text{B–Kt5}}{\text{P–QR3}}$	4 $\frac{\text{B–R4}}{\text{Kt–B3}}$

5 $\frac{\text{0–0}}{\text{B–K2}}$ 6 $\frac{\text{R–K1}}{\text{P–QKt4}}$ 7 $\frac{\text{B–Kt3}}{\text{0–0}}$ 8 $\frac{\text{P–Q4}}{}$ (Avoiding the

Marshall. Now I did not want to allow 8 $\dfrac{\quad}{P\times P}$ 9 $\dfrac{P\text{-}K5}{\quad}$, or to play the orthodox P–Q3 transposing to lines with which I was not familiar, so I settled for Kt × QP; since 9 $\dfrac{Kt\times P}{Kt\times B}$ was satisfactory enough). There followed 8 $\dfrac{\quad}{Kt\times QP}$ 9 $\dfrac{B\times P\ ch.}{R\times B}$ 10 $\dfrac{Kt\times P}{Kt\text{-}K3}$ ($\dfrac{\quad}{Kt\text{-}B3}$ is worse) 11 $\dfrac{Kt\times R}{K\times Kt}$ 12 $\dfrac{P\text{-}K5}{\quad}$ and the Kt cannot be moved because of Q–B3 ch.

Finally I should add that one of the games in this chapter is against my old friend of Cambridge days and President of the BCF, P. S. Milner-Barry, CB, OBE. We have played several times and never had a dull game. Two of his wins against me have been published, so I am sure he will not mind one of mine. But our first encounter in 1926 is worth recalling. I had been impressed by Alekhine's magnificent notes to the 1922 Hastings International Congress and had studied his lengthy analysis of the Möller Defence to the Ruy Lopez. Milner-Barry, as a result of our game, also became a convert to this rarely-played defence, but it was not until Margate 1935 that he was able to unleash it on no less an opponent than Capablanca. But the probability is that Capablanca also knew Alekhine's analysis, for he unerringly laid his finger upon the flaw in it, and I well remember Milner-Barry ruefully telling me how Capablanca had 'bust it'. This little bit of chess history will be found in the chapter on the Möller Defence.

BRITISH CHAMPIONSHIP, 1926

White: R. P. Michell

1 P–Q4	Kt–KB3	9 B×P	Kt–Q4
2 P–QB4	P–K3	10 B×B	Q×B
3 Kt–QB3	P–Q4	11 Kt–K4	....
4 B–Kt5	B–K2		
5 P–K3	QKt–Q2		
6 Kt–B3	0–0		
7 R–B1	P–B3		
8 B–Q3	P×P		

This was the popular move in the 1920s in this standard position. Nowadays the older move 0–0 is preferred, and after Kt × Kt; 12 R × Kt, P–K4;

White has a choice of P×P, Q–B2, Q–Kt1 and B–Kt3.

11 ....   P–K4

I had prepared this pawn sacrifice earlier in 1926, and was able to play it twice in the British Championship, getting a won game also against M. E. Goldstein.

12 P×P   ....

The Goldstein game continued 12 Kt×P, Kt×Kt; 13 P×Kt, Q×P; 14 B×Kt, P×B; 15 Kt–B3, B–K3; 16 0–0, QR–B1; 17 Q–R4, R–B5.

12 ....   QKt×P
13 B×Kt   P×B
14 Kt–B3   ....

Black has sufficient counter-play after 14 Q×P, Kt×Kt ch.; 15 P×Kt, B–K3.

14 ....   B–Kt5

15 Kt×P	Q–Q3
16 0–0	QR–Q1
17 Kt–B4	Q–KR3
18 Q–K2	B×Kt
19 P×B	P–KKt4

20 Kt–Kt2   ....

He loses a piece after 20 Q–Kt5, Kt×P ch.; 21 K–Kt2, Kt–R5 ch.

20 ....   R–Q7
           Resigns

Black: F. Parr

1 P–K4	P–QB4
2 Kt–KB3	Kt–KB3
3 P–K5	Kt–Q4
4 Kt–B3	P–K3
5 Kt×Kt	P×Kt
6 P–Q4	P–Q3
7 B–Q3	....

7 B–Kt5 ch., 7 B–KKt5, and 7 P×P have all been tried for White here. Probably 7 B–Kt5 ch. is best.

7	P–B5
8 B–K2	Kt–QB3
9 0–0	B–K3

10 B–B4	B–K2
11 Q–Q2	0–0
12 QR–K1	P–QKt4
13 Kt–Kt5	B–B4

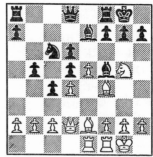

14 P–KKt4   ....

This leads to a lively knockabout.

14	B×BP
15 P–K6	P–B3
16 Kt–B7	Q–B2
17 Q×B	Kt×P
18 Q–Q2	Kt×P
19 Q×P	K×Kt
20 B–Q3	....

Black has no answer to this. P×B allows 21 Q×Kt ch., K–K1; 22 B×P, and Q–Q2 allows 21 B–B5.

20	R–R1
21 R×Kt	QR–K1

This rook would have been loose if he had allowed R×P dis. ch.

22 R×P double ch. *Resigns*

BRITISH CHAMPIONSHIP, 1960

Black: D. B. Pritchard

1 P–K4	P–K4
2 Kt–KB3	Kt–KB3
3 P–Q4	P×P
4 P–K5	Kt–K5
5 Q×P	P–Q4
6 P×P e.p.	Kt×QP
7 Kt–B3	Kt–B3
8 Q–KB4	P–KKt3

B–B4 is answered by B–Kt5.

9 P–KR4	P–KR4
10 B–K3	B–Kt2
11 0–0–0	B–K3

Not liking Q–B3; 12 Q×Q, B×Q; 13 B–KB4 (or B5).

12 B–Kt5	Q–B3
13 B×Kt ch.	P×B

14 R×Kt   ....

A positional sacrifice of the exchange which must be accepted (Q×Q; R×B ch.).

14	P×R
15 Q×P	B–Q4
16 Q–Kt4	P–R4
17 Q–R3	B×Kt
18 P×B	0–0–0
19 Q×P	B–R3
20 Q–R6 ch.	K–Q2

K–Kt1 leads to the same result.

21 Q–R7 ch.   K–B1

Forced, for if he goes on the K–file 22 B×B, R×B; 23 Q–K3 ch., loses a rook.

22 Kt–R4	B×B ch.
23 P×B	R–Q3

24 P–KB4   ....
There is no need to hurry.
24 ....   K–Q1
25 Kt–B5   K–K1
26 Kt–K4   *Resigns*

BRITISH CHAMPIONSHIP, 1965

Black: Dr J. M. Aitken

1 Kt–KB3	P–Q4
2 P–B4	P–QB3
3 P–Q4	Kt–B3
4 P–KKt3	B–B4
5 B–Kt2	QKt–Q2
6 Kt–B3	P–K3
7 0–0	P–KR3
8 Kt–Q2	P–B4

This premature attempt to seize the initiative is the cause of all Black's troubles. The game continues harmoniously to its end.

9 BP×P	BP×P
10 P×P	B×P
11 Kt–Kt5	Q–Kt3
12 Q–R4	B–QB4

Black cannot play Kt–B4 because of Kt–B7 double check and Kt×R.

13 P–QKt4	B–K2
14 B–Kt2	P–R3
15 Kt×P	Q×P
16 Q×Q	B×Q
17 Kt×B	P×Kt
18 Kt–K4	R–QKt1

0–0–0 would be too dangerous.

19 QR–Kt1	B–K2
20 KR–Q1	Kt×Kt

P–QKt4 would be answered by Kt–Q6 ch. 0–0 allows Kt×Kt, Kt×Kt; B–K5.

21 B×Kt   B–B3

Kt–B4 would be answered by B×KKtP. Kt–B3 allows B–Kt6 ch., K–B1; B–K5.

23 Q–B   ....
22 B–R3   B–K2
23 B–Kt6 ch. K–Q1

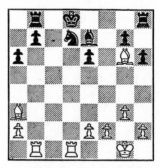

K–B1; 24 R×Kt, B×B;

25 QR×P, R×R; 26 R×R, K–Kt1; 27 R–Kt8 ch., B–B1; 28 P–Kt4 would have led eventually to the black R committing hara-kiri.

24 R×Kt ch. K×R
25 R–Q1 ch. *Resigns*
A simple and satisfying, because logical, conclusion.

HASTINGS CHRISTMAS CONGRESS, 1952–3

White: E. G. Sergeant

1 P–K4	P–K4
2 Kt–KB3	Kt–QB3
3 B–Kt5	P–QR3
4 B–R4	Kt–B3
5 0–0	B–K2
6 P–Q3	....

Sergeant was fond of this quiet move, and sometimes played it a move earlier (the Anderssen variation).

6	P–QKt4
7 B–Kt3	P–Q3
8 P–B3	0–0
9 QKt–Q2	Kt–QR4
10 B–B2	P–B4
11 R–K1	Kt–B3
12 Kt–B1	R–K1
13 Kt–K3	B–B1
14 P–KR3	B–Kt2
15 Kt–B5	Kt–K2
16 P–KKt4	Kt–Kt3
17 P–QR4	P–Q4
18 P×KtP	P×KtP
19 B–Kt5	P–R3
20 R×R	B×R
21 B–Q2	....

21	P–B5

A good example of hitting the base of a pawn chain. White's weakness on the long diagonal becomes apparent.

22 P–Kt5	P×QP
23 B×P	P×KP
24 B×KtP	P×Kt
25 P×Kt	Q×P
26 B×R	Q×Kt
27 K–R2	P–K5
28 B–K3	Q–K4 ch.
29 K–R1	B–Q3
Resigns	

HASTINGS CHRISTMAS CONGRESS, 1957–8

Black: A. Y. Green

1 P–QB4	Kt–KB3	16 Q–K4	P–KKt3
2 Kt–QB3	P–K3	17 Q–R4	Q–Q1
3 P–K4	P–Q4	18 Q–B2	B×Kt
4 P–K5	P–Q5	19 P×B	P–B5

Kt–Kt1 is also playable.

5 P×Kt	P×Kt
6 KtP×P	Q×P
7 P–Q4	P–B4
8 Kt–B3	P–KR3

This move is unnecessary. Black should play P×P.

9 B–Q3	Kt–B3
10 0–0	B–K2
11 Q–K2	0–0

Not liking 11 . . . ., P×P; 12 P×P, Kt×P; 13 Kt×Kt, Q×Kt; 14 B–Kt2.

12 P–Q5	Kt–R4
13 Kt–K5	B–Q3
14 P–B4	P×P
15 P×P	R–K1

Allowing the White queen a useful manoeuvre.

Black probably relied on this move since White cannot play B×KtP because of Q–Kt3 ch.

20 P–K6	R–K2

An alternative was to sacrifice his bishop for the two pawns.

21 B×KtP	P×B
22 Q×P ch.	R–Kt2
23 Q–B5	. . . .

Black is lost. The rest is easy.

23	Q–Kt3 ch.
24 K–R1	B×P
25 P×B	Q–B3
26 R–B3	Q–K1
27 B×P	Q–Kt3
28 B×R	Q×Q
29 R×Q	*Resigns*

HASTINGS CHRISTMAS CONGRESS, 1961–2

Black: P. C. Gibbs

1 P–QB4	P–KKt3
2 Kt–QB3	Kt–KB3
3 P–K4	P–Q3
4 P–Q4	B–Kt2
5 B–K2	0–0
6 B–Kt5	P–B4
7 P–Q5	P–K3
8 Kt–B3	P×P
9 Kt×P	. . . .

Capturing with the piece gives advantages to both White and Black. Now Q–R4 ch. would be answered by P–Kt4 when the Black queen would have to retreat again.

9	R–K1
10 Kt–Q2	Kt–B3
11 0–0	P–KR3

12 Kt×Kt ch.	B×Kt	25 P×P	Q×P
13 B×P	B×P	26 R×Kt	P×R
14 R–Kt1	B–B3	27 R×P ch.	R×R
15 P–B4	Kt–Q5	28 Kt–K6 ch.	Q×Kt
16 B–Kt4	P–Kt3	29 Q×Q	R×P
17 B×B	R×B	30 Q×P ch.	K–Kt2
18 Q–Kt4	B–Kt2		
19 B×B	K×B		
20 P–B5	Q–B3		
21 Kt–B3	R–B2		
22 QR–Q1	QR–K2		
23 Kt–Kt5	R–KR1		

Black is running short of moves. He must maintain a rook on the second rank against White's P×P.

24 P–KR4   ....

Now the threat is P–K5 and if P×P; Kt–K4, or if R×P; P×P.

24 ....   K–B1

A mistake in time trouble. Probably he didn't like the look of K–Q1; 31 P–K5, but R(R5)–B5 would then threaten an immediate draw, so against K–Q1 White would eat up Black's remaining pawns beginning 31 Q–Kt8 ch., K–K2; 32 Q×P ch., etc.

31 Q–Kt3 ch. K–B3
32 Q×R ch. and Black resigned three moves later when the time control had been reached.

HASTINGS CHRISTMAS CONGRESS, 1962–3

White: P. S. Milner-Barry

1 P–K4	P–K4	5 Kt–B3	....
2 P–KB4	P×P		
3 Kt–KB3	P–Q4		
4 P×P	Kt–KB3		

Here White may also try P–B4 or B–Kt5 ch.

5 ....   Kt×P

6 Kt×Kt   ....

Slightly more in keeping with the opening might be B–B4, Kt×Kt; 7 KtP×Kt, B–Q3.

6	Q×Kt
7 B–K2	Kt–B3
8 P–Q4	B–KKt5
9 0–0	0–0–0
10 P–B3	B–Q3
11 P–Kt4	KR–K1
12 P–QR3	....

White's troubles spring from this quiet move, so unlike Milner-Barry's normal attacking style.

12	Q–K3
13 B–Q3	B–KB4
14 B×B	Q×B

With the exchange of his good bishop White's position has worsened.

15 R–R2	P–KKt4
16 QR–KB2	P–Kt5
17 Kt–K1	P–B6

Already B×P ch. is threatened.

18 P×P	P–Kt6
19 P×P	B×P
20 R–KKt2	B×Kt

It was not easy to make this exchange as the bishop seems so much stronger than the knight, but as a result of it the Black knight becomes dominant.

21 R×B	Kt–K4
22 R–B1	R–Kt1
23 Q–K2	Kt–Q6
24 R–Q1	R×R ch.
25 Q×R	R–Q3
26 Q–Kt8 ch.	K–Q2
27 B–Kt5	R–Kt3
28 Q–Q8 ch.	K–B3
29 P–Q5 ch.	K–Kt3
30 R×Kt	Q×R

And Black won. The game ended

31	$\dfrac{\text{K–B2}}{\text{Q–B7 ch.}}$	32	$\dfrac{\text{K–B1}}{\text{Q×P}}$
33	$\dfrac{\text{K–B2}}{\text{Q–Kt7 ch.}}$	34	$\dfrac{\text{K–B1}}{\text{Q×RP}}$
35	$\dfrac{\text{K–B2}}{\text{Q–Kt7 ch.}}$	36	$\dfrac{\text{K–B1}}{\text{Q×P}}$
37	$\dfrac{\text{B–K3 ch.}}{\text{K–R3}}$	38	$\dfrac{\text{Q×P}}{\text{Q–Kt4 ch.}}$
39	$\dfrac{\text{K–B2}}{\text{Q–Kt7 ch.}}$	40	$\dfrac{\text{K–B1}}{\text{Q–Kt7 ch.}}$
41	$\dfrac{\text{K–K1}}{\text{Q–Kt6 ch.}}$		*Resigns*

HASTINGS CHRISTMAS CONGRESS, 1965–6

White: W. Schmidt

1 P–K4	P–K4
2 Kt–QB3	Kt–KB3
3 P–KKt3	P–Q4
4 P×P	B–QB4

I first tried this gambit against Dr D. J. P. Gray in the 1962 Devon Championship. The game continued

5	$\dfrac{\text{B–Kt2}}{\text{P–B3}}$	6	$\dfrac{\text{P×P}}{\text{Kt×P}}$

7 $\dfrac{\text{P–Q3}}{\text{B–KKt5}}$ 8 $\dfrac{\text{Kt–B3}}{\text{P–K5}}$

9 $\dfrac{\text{Kt}\times\text{P}}{\text{Kt}\times\text{Kt}}$ 10 $\dfrac{\text{P}\times\text{Kt}}{\text{Q}\times\text{Q ch.}}$

11 $\dfrac{\text{K}\times\text{Q}}{\text{0–0–0 ch.}}$ 12 $\dfrac{\text{K–K1}}{\text{Kt–Kt5}}$

13 $\dfrac{\text{K–K2}}{\text{Kt}\times\text{BP}}$ 14 $\dfrac{\text{R–QKt1}}{\text{Kt–Q5 ch.}}$

15 $\dfrac{\text{K–K3}}{\text{Kt}\times\text{Kt dis. ch.}}$

16 $\dfrac{\text{K–B4}}{\text{P–B4}}$ 17 $\dfrac{\text{B}\times\text{Kt}}{\text{P- Kt4 ch.}}$

Resigns.

12 P–KKt4	P–KR4
13 P–Kt5	Kt–Q4
14 Kt–K4	....

5 B–Kt2	P–B3	14	Kt×P ch.
6 P×P	Kt×P	15 Q×Kt	B×B
7 KKt–K2	B–KKt5	16 Kt(K2)–B3	Kt–Kt5
8 P–KR3	B–K3	17 Q–K2	Kt×P ch.
9 P–Q3	Q–Q2	18 K–B1	B–Kt3
10 B–Kt5	P–KR3	19 R–Q1	B–B5
11 B–K3	Kt–Q5	And Black won.	

WEST OF ENGLAND CHAMPIONSHIP, 1954

White: R. M. Bruce

1 Kt–KB3	P–Q4
2 P–QB4	P–K3
3 P–KKt3	P×P
4 B–Kt2	Kt–Q2
5 Q–R4	P–QR3
6 Q×BP	KKt–B3
7 0–0	B–K2
8 P–Q4	P–QKt4
9 Q–B6	....

The quiet retreat 9 Q–B2 is probably better. Black later gains a move by attacking the Queen.

9	R–R2

Much better than 9 ...., R–Kt1 when Black has trouble with the White QB.

10 B–B4	B–Kt2
11 Q–B1	....

If White captures the BP with Q or B he loses a piece. In this variation Black has now equalised.

11	P–B4
12 P×P	B×P
13 Kt–B3	0–0

14 Kt–K5	B×B
15 K×B	Q–R1 ch.
16 P–B3	R–B1
17 Q–Q1	Kt×Kt
18 B×Kt	R–Q2
19 Q–Kt3	Kt–Kt5
20 B–B4	P–K4
21 P–KR3	....

21	Kt–R7

This seemed to give a better attacking chance than P×B; 22 P×Kt, or Kt–K6 ch.; 22 B×Kt, B×B; 23 QR–Q1.

22 K×Kt	....

This at least is forced.

22	P×B
23 P–Kt4	R–Q7
24 QR–Q1	R(B1)–Q1
25 P–R3	Q–B3
26 R×R	R×R
27 P–KR4	Q–R3
28 K–R3	B–K2
29 P–R5	Q–Kt4
30 K–Kt2	Q–R5
32 R–KR1	Q–Kt6 ch.
32 K–B1	B–R5
	Resigns

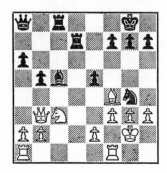

WEST OF ENGLAND CHAMPIONSHIP, 1962

White: F. E. A. Kitto

1 P–K4	P–K4
2 Kt–QB3	Kt–KB3
3 P–B4	P–Q4
4 P×KP	Kt×P
5 Q–B3	Kt–B3
6 B–Kt5	Kt×Kt
7 B×Kt ch.	....

Varying from the usual 7 KtP×Kt, Q–R5 ch.; 8 P–Kt3, Q–K5 ch.

7	P×B
8 Q×Kt	Q–R5 ch.
9 P–Kt3	....

K–B1 would have been better.

9	Q–K5 ch.
10 K–B2	P–QB4

11 Kt–B3	P–Q5
12 Q–Kt3	B–K3
13 Q–R4 ch.	B–Q2
14 Q–Kt3	B–B3
15 R–K1	Q–B4
16 P–K6	0–0–0
17 P–K7	B×P
18 R×B	P–B5
19 Q–R3	KR–K1
	Resigns

See diagram opposite.

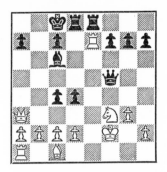

White is a piece to the good, but quite helpless.

COUNTIES CHAMPIONSHIP, 1964

DEVON *v.* SOMERSET

White: R. H. Northage

1 P–K4	P–K4
2 B–B4	Kt–KB3
3 Kt–KB3	Kt–B3
4 Kt–Kt5	P–Q4
5 P×P	Kt–QR4
6 B–Kt5 ch.	P–B3
7 P×P	P×P
8 B–K2	P–KR3
9 Kt–KB3	P–K5
10 Kt–K5	Q–Q5

This is not so good as the usual B–Q3, but can lead to more involved positions.

11 Kt–Kt4	....

Not so good as P–KB4, B–QB4; 12 R–B1 when Black has prevented White castling but has to start retreating with his queen and bishop.

11	B×Kt
12 B×B	P–K6
13 P–KB3	....

Bird advised B–K2 here; B–B3 is also possible.

E

13	Kt×B
14 P×Kt	0–0–0

Black has a won game, but some interesting play remains.

15 P–Q3	B–Kt5 ch.

Here, for example, Black would be wrong to play P–K7; 16 Q×P, B–Kt5 ch.; 17 K–Q1.

16 P–B3	P–K7
17 Q–B2	Q×KtP
18 B–K3	KR–K1
19 B×QRP	B–Q3
20 B–B2	....

Against the threatened B×P.

20	Q×P
21 R–Kt1	Q–R6
22 Q–R4	Q×QP
23 B–Q4	B×P
24 R×P	B–Kt6 ch.

Resigns

WARD–HIGGS CORRESPONDENCE, 1964–5

DEVON *v.* SUFFOLK

Black: P. G. Markwell

1 P–K4	P–K4	15 B–Q2	P–QKt3
2 Kt–KB3	Kt–QB3	16 Q–K2	B–B4
3 B–B4	B–B4	17 R–K1	P–B5
4 P–B3	Kt–B3		

B × R is answered by Q × B, and R–K1 by B–Kt5.

5 P–Q4	P × P
6 P × P	B–Kt5 ch.
7 Kt–B3	Kt × P
8 0–0	B × Kt
9 P–Q5	B–B3

A standard move in this variation of the Möller Attack. Black may also play Kt–K4, which I played against Milner-Barry in the 1951 British Championship. The game continued 10 $\frac{\text{Q–K2}}{\text{0–0}}$ (more usual is P × B for White)

11 $\frac{\text{P × B}}{\text{Kt × Kt ch.}}$ 12 $\frac{\text{Q × Kt}}{\text{Q–R5}}$

13 $\frac{\text{R–K1}}{\text{Kt–B3}}$ 14 $\frac{\text{B–Q3}}{\text{P–Q3}}$

with a good game for Black.

10 R–K1	0–0

Kt–K2; 11 R × Kt, P–Q3 is more usual.

11 R × Kt	Kt–R4

This does not turn out well. However, Kt–K2 would allow White an attack commencing with P–KKt4.

12 B–Q3	P–Q3
13 P–KKt4	P–B4
14 P–Kt5	B–K2

18 B–B2	R–K1
19 B–R4	B–Q2
20 B × B	Q × B

Black's last three moves have been forced.

21 Kt–R4	....

Not R × B because of Q–Kt5 ch.

21	K–B1
22 Q–B3	K–Kt1

To meet the threat of P–Kt6.

13 Q–K3	K–B1

The White Q has completed a triangulation on to a Black square.

24 B–B3	Kt–Kt2

Black has little he can do.

25 Q–Q4	P–B3
26 R–K6	Kt–B4
27 P × P	B × P
28 R × B ch.	*Resigns*

After P × R, mate follows with 29 Q × P ch., Q–B2; 30 Kt–Kt6 ch, P × Kt; 31 Q–R8 ch. Q–Kt1; 32 Q–R6 ch., K–B2; 33 Q–B4 mate.

The game was awarded the Boyd Prize for the best correspondence game in the Counties Championships.

Now follow the five game positions which are referred to at the beginning of this chapter.

BRITISH CHAMPIONSHIP,
1946

Black: R. F. Combe

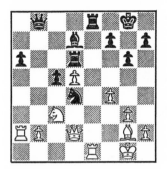

Position after White's 28th
move Kt–B3.

28	B–R6
29 Kt–K4	B×B
30 K×B	R×Kt
31 R×R	Q–Kt6
32 R×Kt	P×R
33 R–R5	R×P
34 R×P	Q–Kt2
35 R–R3	R–QKt4 dis. ch.
36 K–R3	R–R4 ch.
37 K–Kt4	P–B4 mate

BCF CONGRESS, 1924,
MAJOR OPEN

Black: O. C. Müller

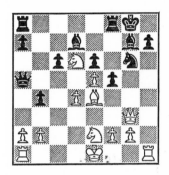

Position after Black's 20th
move Kt×P.

21 0–0–0 ....

The bishop is not wanted for
the attack and is jettisoned.

21 .... P×B

22 K–Kt1 ....

But first White's own position
is secured.

22 .... Q–R3

The queen gets out of play
here.

23 Kt–B1	R–B4
24 R×P	K×R
25 R–R1 ch.	K–Kt1
26 Q×Kt	B–K1
27 Kt×B	R×Kt
28 Q×R ch.	R–B1
29 Q×P ch.	R–B2
30 R–K1	Q–Kt4
31 R×P	Q–Q4
32 Q×Q	P×Q

33 R–K2 and won.

WEST OF ENGLAND
CHAMPIONSHIP, 1948

SECOND GAME OF TIE-
MATCH

White: Capt. P. D. Bolland

Position after White's 17th
move Kt × P. White's king is
precariously placed, but Black
has to meet threats of Kt × R
and Q–K8 mate.

17 ....   Q–Kt5 ch.
18 K–Q1   ....

Q–Q2 allows Q–K2 ch., and
K–B2 allows B–B4 ch.

18 ....   Q–R5 ch.
19 K–B1   ....

Again White has no choice, as
P–Kt3 allows Q–Q2 ch., and
K–K1 allows B–Kt5 ch.

19 ....   B–K2

Since White cannot play Q × B,
Q–B7 mate or Kt × R, B–Kt4
ch.

20 P–QKt3   B–R6 ch.
    Resigns

The knight is lost after all.

BRITISH CHAMPIONSHIP,
1949

White: J. Penrose

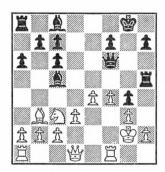

This is really rather a horrid
thing. Black, who has played an
unsound gambit and has now a
lost game, has just played his
queen from Q1 to B3. He has one
hope left. The game ended:

18 Q–K2   R × P ch.
    Resigns

'Your attack had a little more
life than I realised,' ruefully
commented my teen-aged
opponent, whose record series
of championship wins had yet to
begin.

BRITISH CHAMPIONSHIP, 1972

Black: M. J. Corden

What may well turn out to be the last game I shall play in the British Championship had a delightful termination. Take a good look at the position. It is clear that White's king's-side pawns are under attack and are very weak. Do you see anything else?

The game continued:
33 R(Q6)–Q4 . . . .

Hoping that after R × R; 34 Q × R, Q × Q; 35 R × Q, the endgame would be playable.
33 . . . .   R–B6
34 R–Q7   . . . .

Saving the KRP by the reply R × P ch. However my opponent took the QRP instead, leaving me no option but to resign!

7 The Möller Defence to the Ruy Lopez

$$1\ \frac{P\text{–}K4}{P\text{–}K4}\quad 2\ \frac{Kt\text{–}KB3}{Kt\text{–}QB3}\quad 3\ \frac{B\text{–}Kt5}{P\text{–}QR3}\quad 4\ \frac{B\text{–}R4}{Kt\text{–}B3}\quad 5\ \frac{0\text{–}0}{B\text{–}B4}$$

L. W. Barden, in his great work on the Ruy Lopez, devotes little space to this defence, saying that it 'is out of fashion and White has several methods of obtaining a positional advantage'. He then considers the variations:

$$6\ \frac{P\text{–}B3}{B\text{–}R2}\quad 7\ \frac{P\text{-}Q4}{P\text{–}QKt4}\quad 8\ \frac{B\text{–}Kt3}{Q\text{–}K2}\quad \text{and}$$

$$6\ \frac{P\text{–}B3}{B\text{–}R2}\quad 7\ \frac{P\text{–}Q4}{0\text{–}0}\quad 8\ \frac{P\times P}{KKt\times P}\quad 9\ \frac{Q\text{–}Q5}{Kt\text{–}B4}\quad 10\ \frac{B\text{–}B2}{}.$$

Alekhine's advocacy of the variation however, was based upon Black playing $7\ \frac{}{Kt\times KP}$. Here is his game with Yates in the Hastings International Tournament played in September 1922, together with his own notes.

White: F. D. Yates
Black: A. Alekhine

1 P–K4	P–K4
2 Kt–KB3	Kt–QB3
3 B–Kt5	P–QR3
4 B–R4	Kt–B3
5 0–0	B–B4

This move was recommended some twenty years ago by the Danish Master, Möller, but his analysis was neither thorough nor very correct. In my opinion it is due to this fact alone, that the defence has been so rarely adopted in master practice. As far as I am concerned I believe in its future and this game goes to confirm its value.

6 P–B3 ....

Probably the best move here. If 6 Kt×P then 6 ...., Kt×Kt; 7 P–Q4, Kt×P; 8 R–K1, B–K2; 9 R×Kt, Kt–Kt3 with equality

(Möller). Mr Burn suggests 6
R–K1, Kt–KKt5; 7 R–K2 (not
7 P–Q4 because of 7 . . . ., P×P;
8 Kt×P, Kt×Kt; 9 Q×KKt,
0–0; and Black has the better
game), Kt–Q5; 8 Kt×Kt,
B×Kt; 9 P–KR3, Kt×P; 10
R×Kt, B×R ch.; 11 K×B,
Q–R5 ch.; 12 K–Kt1, Q×KP;
13 Kt–B3 and White for
preference.

| 6 . . . . | B–R2 |
| 7 P–Q4 | . . . . |

If 7 R–K1 then Black obtains
the advantage by the following
sacrificial combinations:

7 . . . ., Kt–KKt5; 8 P–Q4 (if
8 R–K2, Q–B3; 9 P–KR3, P–KR4
etc.), P×P; 9 P×P (or 9 P–KR3,
KKt–K4; 10 Kt×Kt, Kt×Kt;
11 P×P, Kt–Kt3; followed by
12 . . . ., 0–0 with equality),
Kt×QP!! 10 Kt×Kt, Q–R5;
11 B–K3 (if 11 Kt–B3 then mate
follows in 3 moves), Q×RP ch.;
12 K–B1, Q–R8 ch.; 13 K–K2,
Q×P; etc., with three pawns for
the piece and a very powerful
attack besides.

7	Kt×KP
8 Q–K2	P–B4
9 P×P	0–0
10 QKt–Q2	P–Q4
11 P×P e.p.	Kt ×QP
12 B–Kt3 ch.	

If 12 B×Kt, P×B; Black
would have sufficient compensation with the two bishops
and his general attacking
position for his unfavourable
pawn position.

| 12 . . . . | K–R1 |
| 13 Kt–B4 | P–B5 |

Restraining the action of the
adversary's pieces whilst
enlarging that of his own – the
maximum that one can expect
from a positional move.

| 14 QKt–K5 | Kt×Kt |
| 15 Kt×Kt | Q–Kt4 |

The signal of attack, and at
the same time a defence against
the threat of 16 Q–R5, Q–B3;
17 B×P, etc.

16 B–Q2	B–R6
17 B–Q5	QR–K1
18 QR–K1	R–K3

A very strong move which
should give Black the advantage.
Not only does it fend off the
threat of 19 Kt–B7 ch., but it
threatens in its turn the doubling
of the rooks on the king's file
with decisive pressure.

| 19 Q–Q3 | . . . . |

The only move. If instead 19
K–R1 then simply 19 . . . .,
KR–K1; 20 P×B, R×Kt and
wins.

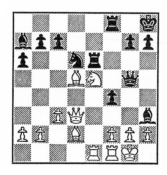

19 . . . .   B–K6

An extraordinary hallucination. Feeling a bit off for play that day this move literally fascinated me! Instead of this unsound combination I could have won a pawn by simply playing 19 . . . ., B×P; 20 B×B (20 P–KR4?, B×R dis. ch.), R×Kt etc.

20 B×B   . . . .

This move is not bad, but does not secure any advantage, whilst 20 P×B, P–B6; 21 B×BP, R×B; 22 Q–K2!, R×R ch.; 23 R×R, would leave him with an extra pawn. All the same it is doubtful whether this material gain would have led to victory, for after 23 . . . ., Q–K2; 24 Kt–B3 (or 24 Q–R5, B–B4;), B–Kt5; and Black undoubtedly maintains the superior position.

20 . . . .   R×Kt
21 B–B1   B–Kt5
22 B–B3   KR–K1

Another mistake on this occasion through pressure of time. The correct continuation was 22 . . . ., B×B; 23 Q×B, Q–B4 with a satisfactory game.

23 R×R   R×R
24 B×B   . . . .

White does likewise. 24 P–KKt3 would have won an important pawn.

24 . . . .   Q×B
25 P–KR3   Q–K7

Thus forcing an even game.

Also after 25 . . . ., Q–R5; 26 Q–B3 etc. Black would not have obtained any advantage.

26 Q×Q   R×Q
27 B×P   R×KtP
28 B×Kt   P×B
29 R–Q1   R–Kt3

If 29 . . . ., R×RP; 30 R×P, P–R3; 31 R–QKt6 etc., with an immediate liquidation of forces.

30 R–Q4   R–B3
31 P–QR4   K–Kt1
32 K–B1   K–B2
33 K–K2   K–K3
34 K–Q3   . . . .

After this White has nothing further to fear and the game could now safely be abandoned as drawn.

34 . . . .   R–B4
35 R–QKt4   R–Q4 ch.
36 K–K3   R–K4 ch.
37 K–Q3   . . . .

In this position White has only to avoid the exchange of rooks. For example, 37 R–K4, K–Q4!; 38 R×R ch., P×R; 39 K–Q3, P–K5 ch. winning.

37 . . . .   R–KKt4
38 P–Kt3   P–Kt4
39 P×P   P×P
40 R–K4 ch.   K–Q4
41 R–KB4   K–B4
42 R–B7   R–Kt3
43 R–B7 ch.   K–Q4
44 R–Kt7   K–B3
45 R–K7   R–Kt4
          Drawn.

By the time the 1925 *Modern Chess Openings* had appeared in print, two more Alekhine games had appeared, in each of which White had played 6 Kt×P instead of 6 P–B3. One was Takacs–Alekhine, Vienna, 1922, which continued:

6 $\dfrac{\text{Kt}\times\text{P}}{\text{Kt}\times\text{Kt}}$ 7 $\dfrac{\text{P–Q4}}{\text{Kt}\times\text{P}}$ 8 $\dfrac{\text{Q–K2}}{\text{B–K2}}$ 9 $\dfrac{\text{Q}\times\text{Kt}}{\text{Kt–Kt3}}$

10 $\dfrac{\text{P–QB4}}{\text{0–0}}$ 11 $\dfrac{\text{Kt–B3}}{\text{P–KB4}}$ 12 $\dfrac{\text{Q–B3}}{\text{Kt–R5}}$ 13 $\dfrac{\text{Q–Q3}}{}$

with some advantage to White. That this variation is still playable for Black, I showed by scoring my only win against P. H. Clarke in the British Championship at Aberystwyth in 1955. The game is given later.

The other was W. P. Shipley and S. T. Sharp in consultation against Alekhine at Philadelphia in 1924. It went:

6 $\dfrac{\text{Kt}\times\text{P}}{\text{Kt}\times\text{Kt}}$ 7 $\dfrac{\text{P–Q4}}{\text{Kt}\times\text{P}}$ 8 $\dfrac{\text{Q–K2}}{\text{B–K2}}$ 9 $\dfrac{\text{Q}\times\text{Kt}}{\text{Kt–Kt3}}$

10 $\dfrac{\text{P–KB4}}{\text{0–0}}$ 11 $\dfrac{\text{P–B5}}{\text{P–Q4}}$ 12 $\dfrac{\text{Q–Q3}}{\text{Kt–R5}}$ 13 $\dfrac{\text{B–K3}}{\text{B–Kt4}}$

with advantage to Black. Alekhine said that a variant would have been 13 $\dfrac{\text{P–B3}}{\text{B–Kt4}}$ 14 $\dfrac{\text{Kt–Q2}}{\text{Q–B3}}$ also with advantage. My game with Milner-Barry which decided the Cambridge University Championship in 1926 followed this variation to Move 13, when Milner-Barry sought to win a piece by 13 $\dfrac{\text{P–KKt3}}{}$. Here is the game:

White: P. S. Milner-Barry

1 P–K4	P–K4	12 Q–Q3	Kt–R5
2 Kt–KB3	Kt–QB3	13 P–KKt3	P–B4
3 B–Kt5	P–QR3	14 P×Kt	....
4 B–R4	Kt–B3		Not liking 14 P×P, B×P ch.;
5 0–0	B–B4		15 K–R1, P–QKt4; 16 B–Kt3,
6 Kt×P	Kt×Kt		B–Kt2; 17 P×Kt, P–Q5 dis. ch.;
7 P–Q4	Kt×P		18 K–Kt1, Q×P; when Black
8 Q–K2	B–K2		would have a tremendous attack.
9 Q×Kt	Kt–Kt3	14	P–QKt4
10 P–KB4	0–0	15 B–Kt3	P–B5
11 P–B5	P–Q4	16 Q–KB3	P×B

F

There doesn't seem to be any particular hurry to make this capture.

| 17 RP×P | B×RP |
| 18 Kt–B3 | B–Kt2 |

This is a miserable square for the bishop. 18 ...., P–Kt5 would have been better.

19 B–B4	R–K1
20 K–R1	B–KB3
21 QR–Q1	Q–Q2
22 Q–Kt4	QR–B1
23 R–Q2	R–B3
24 Kt–K2	R–K5
25 P–B3	P–Kt5
26 Kt–Kt3	P×P

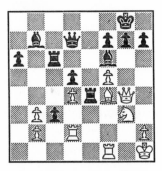

A complex position. I think White should have tried 27 P×P, R×BP; 28 Kt–R5, when Black's position may not be defensible.

| 27 Kt×R | P×R |

27 ...., P×Kt; should have been played when Black's QB would enter the game with devastating effect.

| 28 Kt×B ch. | R×Kt |
| 29 B–K5 | .... |

Tempting, but bad. 29 B×P would probably have led to a draw.

| 29 .... | P=Q |

White must have overlooked this resource.

| 30 Q×Q | R×P |
| 31 R–K1 | .... |

Naturally not 31 R–Kt1 because of 31 ...., R×B.

31	R–Kt4
32 B–B4	R–Kt3
33 Q–R5	R–K3
34 R–KKt1	P–B3
35 B–R6	R–K2
36 Q–B3	Q–K3
37 Q–Kt3	Q–K5 ch.
38 R–Kt2	Q–K8 ch.
39 R–Kt1	Q–K5 ch.
40 R–Kt2	Q–K8 ch.

To reach the time control.

41 R–Kt1	Q×Q
42 R×Q	K–B1
43 B–Q2	K–B2
44 B–Kt4	R–K3
45 R–QB3	B–B3
46 R–B5	P–Kt4
47 K–Kt2	K–Kt3
48 R–B1	B–Kt4
49 R–B5	....

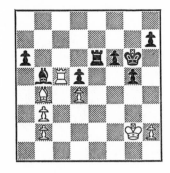

Gives Black the chance to make a little combination.

49	R–K7 ch.
50 K–Kt1	. . . .

The only square to preserve any chance.

50	R × KtP
51 R × P	R–Kt7 ch.
52 K × R	. . . .

52 K–R1 would have led to 52 . . . ., B–B3; 53 R–Q6, B–B6;

54 P–R3, P–KR4; followed by . . . ., P–Kt5 and . . . ., P–Kt6.

52	B–B3
53 K–Kt3	B × R
54 B–Q2	B × P
55 B–B3	B–Q4
56 B–Q2	P–B4
57 P–R4	P–B5 ch.
58 K–R3	P–R3
59 K–Kt4	P–R4 ch.
	Resigns

Now I come to Capablanca's refutation of the variation, played at Margate in 1935.

White: J. R. Capablanca
Black: P. S. Milner-Barry

1 P–K4	P–K4
2 Kt–KB3	Kt–QB3
3 B–Kt5	P–QR3
4 B–R4	Kt–B3
5 0–0	B–B4
6 P–B3	B–R2
7 P–Q4	Kt × KP
8 R–K1	. . . .

Keres, in his book on the openings, shows that Yates' move of 8 Q–K2 had continued to hold favour and had indeed been played by Alekhine himself in a game against Steiner in 1932 which continued 8 . . . ., P–B4; 9 P × P, 0–0; 10 B–Kt3 ch., K–R1; 11 QKt–Q2 when Black should have played 11 . . . ., P–Q4 instead of 11 . . . ., Q–K1. For the whole game see Alekhine's *My Best Games of Chess 1924–1937*.

8	P–B4

9 QKt–Q2	. . . .

In an earlier round E. G. Sergeant had played 9 R × Kt, P × R; 10 B–KKt5, Kt–K2; 11 Kt × P, 0–0; 12 Kt–Q2, P–Q4; 13 Kt × P, B–K3; 14 Kt–Kt3, when Milner-Barry could have equalised with 14 Q–Q3 instead of losing by 14 . . . ., P–R3; 15 B × Kt, Q × B; 16 Kt–Kt6. A very interesting discovery in this variation is 12 B × P!, B × B; 13 Q–Kt3 ch., K–R1; 14 Kt–B7 ch., R × Kt; 15 Q × R, and White is soon a pawn to the good.

9	0–0
10 Kt × Kt	P × Kt
11 B–KKt5	. . . .

The move which was unconsidered in Möller's original analysis which continued 11 R × P, P–Q3; 12 B × Kt (B–KKt5 was still on), P × B; 13 P × P,

B–KB4; 14 R–K1, B–Kt5 etc.

11 . . . .   Q–K1

12 R×P   P–Q3

13 P×P   Q–Kt3

13 . . . ., B–KB4; was a little better but still left White with the advantage.

14 R–KB4   R×R

15 B×R   B–Kt5

16 Q–Kt3 ch. Q–B2

17 Kt–Kt5   Q×Q

18 B×Q ch. *Resigns*

Since this game 7 . . . ., Kt×KP has been under a cloud, and this explains why it is not considered in Barden's book.

I rashly tried one of the alternatives considered by Barden against E. G. Sergeant in the British Championship in 1956 and was lucky to get away with it!

SERGEANT / THOMAS	1	$\frac{\text{P–K4}}{\text{P–K4}}$	2	$\frac{\text{Kt–KB3}}{\text{Kt–QB3}}$	3	$\frac{\text{B–Kt5}}{\text{P–QR3}}$
4 $\frac{\text{B–R4}}{\text{Kt–B3}}$	5 $\frac{\text{0–0}}{\text{B–B4}}$	6 $\frac{\text{P–B3}}{\text{P–QKt4}}$	7 $\frac{\text{B–Kt3}}{\text{B–R2}}$
8 $\frac{\text{P–Q4}}{\text{Q–K2}}$	9 $\frac{\text{B–Q5}}{}$

(Most unpleasant for Black) 9 $\frac{}{\text{P×P}}$ 10 $\frac{\text{Kt×P}}{}$ (A mistake. 10 P×P would have left White with a tremendous game.)

10 $\frac{}{\text{Kt×B}}$ 11 $\frac{\text{Kt×Kt}}{\text{P×Kt}}$ 12 $\frac{\text{P×Kt}}{\text{0–0}}$ 13 $\frac{\text{P×P}}{\text{Q–B3}}$ and Black won.

A year earlier the Möller had stood me in good stead against P. H. Clarke as follows:

CLARKE / THOMAS	1	$\frac{\text{P–K4}}{\text{P–K4}}$	2	$\frac{\text{Kt–KB3}}{\text{Kt–QB3}}$	3	$\frac{\text{B–Kt5}}{\text{P–QR3}}$
4 $\frac{\text{B–R4}}{\text{Kt–B3}}$	5 $\frac{\text{0–0}}{\text{B–B4}}$	6 $\frac{\text{Kt×P}}{\text{Kt×Kt}}$	7 $\frac{\text{P–Q4}}{\text{Kt×P}}$
8 $\frac{\text{Q–K2}}{\text{B–K2}}$	9 $\frac{\text{Q×Kt}}{\text{Kt–Kt3}}$	10 $\frac{\text{P–QB4}}{\text{0–0}}$	11 $\frac{\text{Kt–B3}}{\text{P–KB4}}$
12 $\frac{\text{Q–Q3}}{\text{P–B5}}$	13 $\frac{\text{P–B3}}{\text{P–Q3}}$	14 $\frac{\text{B–B2}}{\text{B–R5}}$	15 $\frac{\text{B–Q2}}{\text{B–B4}}$
16 $\frac{\text{Kt–K4}}{\text{P–B3}}$	17 $\frac{\text{P–Q5}}{\text{Kt–K4}}$	18 $\frac{\text{Q–Kt3}}{\text{P×P}}$	19 $\frac{\text{P×P}}{\text{B×Kt}}$
20 $\frac{\text{B×B}}{\text{P–QKt4}}$	21 $\frac{\text{B–B3}}{\text{Kt–B5}}$	22 $\frac{\text{Q–B2}}{\text{P–R3}}$	23 $\frac{\text{Q–Q3}}{\text{B–B3}}$

24 $\dfrac{\text{P–QR4}}{\text{Kt}\times\text{P}}$ 25 $\dfrac{\text{B}\times\text{Kt}}{\text{B}\times\text{B}}$ 26 $\dfrac{\text{R–R2}}{\text{B–K4}}$ 27 $\dfrac{\text{P}\times\text{P}}{\text{Q–Kt3 ch.}}$

28 $\dfrac{\text{K–R1}}{\text{Q}\times\text{P}}$ 29 $\dfrac{\text{R–QKt1}}{\text{Q}\times\text{Q}}$ 30 $\dfrac{\text{B}\times\text{Q}}{\text{P–QR4}}$ 31 $\dfrac{\text{B–B2}}{\text{B–B6}}$

32 $\dfrac{\text{P–R4}}{\text{QR–Kt1}}$ 33 $\dfrac{\text{R}\times\text{R}}{\text{R}\times\text{R}}$ 34 $\dfrac{\text{B–R4}}{\text{B–K8}}$ 35 $\dfrac{\text{B–B2}}{\text{K–B2}}$

36 $\dfrac{\text{K–R2}}{\text{B}\times\text{P}}$ 37 $\dfrac{\text{R}\times\text{P}}{\text{B–Kt6 ch.}}$ 38 $\dfrac{\text{K–R3}}{\text{K–B3}}$ 39 $\dfrac{\text{R–R7}}{\text{P–R4}}$

40 $\dfrac{\text{R–Q7}}{\text{R–Kt3}}$ 41 $\dfrac{\text{R–Q8}}{\text{R–R3}}$ 42 $\dfrac{\text{R–QKt8}}{}$

(Here he misses his best move 42 R–K8!) 42 $\dfrac{}{\text{R–R8}}$ 43 $\dfrac{\text{R–Kt1}}{\text{R–R7}}$

44 $\dfrac{\text{B–R7}}{}$ (The bishop was not in such danger as it seemed. If Black captures it, White may contrive perpetual check by continually sacrificing his rook in a stalemate position.)

44 $\dfrac{}{\text{R–R4}}$ 45 $\dfrac{\text{B–Kt8}}{\text{P–Kt4}}$ 46 $\dfrac{\text{B–K6}}{\text{R–R2}}$ 47 $\dfrac{\text{B–B8}}{\text{R–KKt2}}$

48 $\dfrac{\text{R–Kt5}}{\text{P–Kt5 ch.}}$ 49 $\dfrac{\text{P}\times\text{P}}{\text{P}\times\text{P ch.}}$ 50 $\dfrac{\text{B}\times\text{P}}{\text{R–R2 ch.}}$ 51 $\dfrac{\text{B–R5}}{\text{R}\times\text{B ch.}}$

52 $\dfrac{\text{K–Kt4}}{\text{R–Kt4 ch.}}$ 53 $\dfrac{\text{K–B3}}{\text{R–K4}}$ 54 $\dfrac{\text{K–Kt4}}{\text{B–R7}}$ White lost on time.

My optimistic forecast is that the Möller doesn't need an impossible number of new ideas to make it once more a useful surprise weapon for Black.

8 I Play an American Computer

How soon will computers be able to play perfect chess? How good are they at present?

These are questions which are often asked by the chess community, without any definite reply being forthcoming. It is known, for example, that a match took place between an American and a Russian computer (which was won by the latter), and that the former world champion, Botvinnik, has worked on programming chess computers and has published a book on them; also that another former world champion, Euwe, has written on them in Anne Sunnucks' *Encyclopedia of Chess*.

Probably the most prevalent view is that they will one day become very good, but that they are not very good at present.

It was, therefore, with a lot of pleasure and a good deal of excitement that I received an invitation from Mr Marvin Minsky of the Massachusetts Institute of Technology, Cambridge, to play against their computer when I was on a visit to Boston in 1968. I had been told that the MIT computer was considered superior to the Berkeley one which had lost to the Russians, and, when I arrived to play it, I found that it was proudly sporting a cup which it had won at the Boston Chess Club.

It had an elegant television screen on which the game was clearly visible. On a move being typed, the piece in question disappeared from its square and re-appeared in its new one. On the left-hand side of the screen the game score was recorded, but not in the same way as the moves were typed. For example, the first move was typed P–QKt4, but appeared on the screen as P/QKt2–QKt4; the third move B×P was B/QKt2×P/K5.

I was told that I would play against the computer's full tournament programme. In this it considers every single available move, giving each a mathematical evaluation. Then the first sixteen of these are considered in the light of the best play for the next two moves on both sides, and the original evaluation modified accordingly, so that the move finally chosen may have been quite low in the first list. The computer played to a time limit of 40 moves in two hours.

Naturally, I had no idea what I should be up against when the game started, and my reactions are recorded in my notes on the game, which also give the time taken by the computer over each move. My own time was not recorded, but it must have been slightly more than the computer's, as the whole game lasted approximately five hours. I will not spoil things here by relating my discomfiture at the end, but leave it to the notes to explain.

A final invaluable courtesy was extended to me by Mr Minsky in letting me have the 'thoughts' of the computer from moves 3 to 23. Each move occupies a separate sheet of paper which contains references to backward and isolated pawns, the mathematical evaluation of every legal move, analysis of the main variations of the sixteen best moves together with programmed details and time consumed. Naturally to reproduce all of this would be too much, but I have given the analysis of the important possibilities for all of these moves which computer admirers may well find fascinating.

MASSACHUSETTS INSTITUTE OF TECHNOLOGY, 1968

Black: MacHack VI

1 P–QKt4 ....
Partly because it's an interesting opening, and partly hoping the computer hasn't been programmed with it.
1 .... P–K4 (0.58)
2 B–Kt2 B×P (1.09)
Surprisingly giving up the KP. The book move is P–KB3.
3 B×P P–KB3 (0.47)
And now Kt–KB3 is more natural. The computer has not impressed so far.
4 B–Kt2 Kt–B3 (0.53)
5 P–K4 Q–K2 (1.37)

Perhaps it can play good chess after all!
6 Q–B3 P–Q3 (3.12)
Fortunately for me (and as the computer realises), P–Q4 loses a pawn to Q–R5 ch.
7 Kt–B3 Kt–K4 (2.53)
8 Q–Kt3 P–B3 (3.02)
9 P–Q4 Kt–Kt5 (1.46)
10 0–0–0 B–Q2 (4.08)
11 B–K2 QKt–R3 (1.32)
12 B–R5 ch. ....
To weaken the diagonal for my QB.
12 .... P–Kt3 (0.44)

13 B–B3   P–KB4 (2.50)

The start of a faulty combination.

14 Kt–R3   B×Kt (4.12)

Continuing the bad work.

15 B×B   P×P 1.58)

16 B×P   ....

Now it really must castle, with a position weakened by the exchanges. Instead it plays the losing move!

16 ....   P–Q4 (4.05)

17 B×P ch.   ....

Naturally!

17 ....   K–B1 (2.22)

White has a won game. Now to finish it off!

18 B–Kt2   Q–B3 (7.04)

19 B–R3 ch. Kt–K2 (1.12)

20 KR–K1   Kt–Kt1 (3.22)

21 Kt–B4   ....

It seems that Black has no good moves. To my astonishment it finds one.

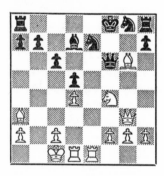

21 ....   R–B1! (3.07)

22 R×Kt   Kt×R (1.11)

23 R–K1   P–B4! (3.11)

24 B–Q3   ....

Not 24 B×BP? R×B.

24 ....   P–Kt3 (6.19)

Another good move. It's not quite so easy to finish off after all.

25 Q–K3   K–B2 (8.15)

This was its longest think.

26 P×P   P–Q5 (3.25)

27 B–B4 ch. K–B1 (4.01)

28 Q–KB3   B–B3 (7.02)

29 Kt–K6 ch. K–B2 (2.18)

30 Kt–B4 dis. ch. K–B1 (2.10)

31 Kt–Kt6 ch. ....

Taking the simplest way to win.

31 ....   K–Kt2 (1.59)

32 Q×Q ch. K×Q (0.53)

33 Kt×Kt   ....

In effect the game is over. But computers are not yet programmed to resign, and probably my friends would not believe I had won unless I delivered checkmate.

33 ....   B×P (2.33)

34 Kt×R   R×Kt (0.44)

35 R–K6 ch. K–Kt4 (1.43)

36 R–K7   ....

Threatening the bishop.

36 ....   B–B6 (4.01)

Noted!

37 B–R6   R–QKt1 (6.45)

Another long think. It is not deterred by the hopelessness of the position.

38 R×QRP   B–K5 (3.10)

39 P×P   R×P (1.23)

40 B–K7 ch. K–B4 (1.36)

41 B–B5   R–QB3 (1.19)

42 B×P   R×P ch. (0.39)

43 K–Q1   K–K3 (1.58)

44 B–Kt5   P–R4 (1.48)
45 B–R4   ....

Now, methinks, it really would save a lot of time if it played R–B5 (or perhaps R×RP).

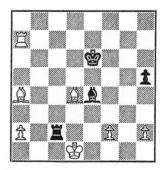

45 ....   R–B5 (0.43)

Played very quickly. It is, in fact, the only good move and I hadn't noticed that it was.

46 B–Kt3   B–B7 ch. (1.34)
Of course!

47 B×B   R×B ch. (0.18)
48 K–K2   R–KR5 (1.23)
49 R–KR7   R×P (0.34)
50 P–R4   P–R5 (0.16)
51 P–R5   R–R6 (0.29)
52 B–Q3   R–R8 (0.45)
53 P–R6   P–R6 (0.30)
54 P–R7   R–R8 (0.58)
55 B–K4   R–R7 ch. (0.31)
56 K–K3   R–R6 ch. (0.30)
57 K–B4   R–R7 (1.28)

58 P=Q   R×P ch. (0.42)

Why does it think this is better than R×Q? Is it losing heart?

59 B–B3   R×B ch. (1.17)
60 K×R   ....

Q×R might be better. Perhaps I am getting tired.

60 ....   K–K4 (0.19)
61 K–K3   P–R7 (0.31)
62 Q–K4 ch.   K–Q3 (0.30)
63 K–Q4   P=Q (0.06)

Played very quickly. It just had to decide which piece to promote to.

64 Q–K5 ch.   K–B3 (0.08)
65 Q–B5 mate.

Although this is a satisfactory concluding move, it was not so satisfactory at the time. I should explain that when I typed my moves for the computer's consideration, I never announced any checks, having been assured that the computer knew perfectly well when it was in check.

Accordingly, for move 65 I just typed Q–B5, and was most disconcerted when it immediately typed back 'Ambiguous'. With a red face I re-typed Q–QB5, whereat it instantly added 'Checkmate'.

EXTRACTS FROM THE COMPUTER'S THOUGHTS FOR MOVES 3 TO 23

The figures give the first evaluation before being revised by analysis in depth. The move finally played has its figure underlined, and it can be seen (Moves 5, 6, 7, 8, 10, 13, 14, etc.) that it was not always thought to be the best at first.

3 795 P–KB3 $\dfrac{\text{B–Q4}}{\text{Kt–B3}}$ $\underline{\text{P–QB3}}$

  765 Kt–KB3 $\dfrac{\text{P–QB3}}{\text{B–B4}}$ $\underline{\text{P–K3}}$

These are certainly two peculiar variations!

4 638 Kt–B3 $\dfrac{\text{P–QB3}}{\text{B–B4}}$ $\underline{\text{P–K3}}$

  617 P–Q4 $\dfrac{\text{P–K3}}{\text{Kt–B3}}$ $\underline{\text{P–QB3}}$

  591 P–Q3 $\dfrac{\text{P–K4}}{\text{Kt–B3}}$ $\underline{\text{P–QB3}}$

5 649 P–Q4 $\dfrac{\text{Q–R5 ch.}}{\text{P–Kt3}}$ $\underline{\text{Q}\times\text{QP}}$

  606 Q–K2 $\dfrac{\text{Kt–QB3}}{\text{P–B4 (a)}}$ $\underline{\text{P–B3}}$

(a) Surprising that it doesn't prefer

   $\overline{\text{B}\times\text{Kt}}$ $\dfrac{\text{B}\times\text{B}}{\text{Q}\times\text{P ch.}}$

  583 P–Q3 $\dfrac{\text{P–QB3}}{\text{B–B4}}$ $\underline{\text{Q–R5 ch.}}$

These variations are not impressive.

6 753 P–Q4 $\dfrac{\text{Q–R5 ch.}}{\text{P–Kt3}}$ $\underline{\text{Q}\times\text{QP}}$

  735 Kt–K4 $\dfrac{\text{Q–QKt3}}{\text{Kt–B3!?}}$ $\underline{\text{P–KB3}}$

  566 P–Q3 $\dfrac{\text{P–QR3}}{\text{B–R4}}$ $\underline{\text{B–B4}}$

7 944 Kt–Q5 $\dfrac{\text{Q–Q3}}{\text{Kt–B3}}$ $\dfrac{\text{Kt–Q5}}{\text{Q–B2}}$ $\dfrac{\text{Kt}\times\text{B}}{\text{Kt}\times\text{Kt}}$

  703 Kt–K4 $\dfrac{\text{Q–R5 ch.}}{\text{Q–B2}}$ $\dfrac{\text{Q}\times\text{Q ch.}}{\text{K}\times\text{Q}}$

648   P–B4 $\dfrac{\text{Kt–Q5}}{\text{Q–B2}}$ $\underline{\text{0–0–0}}$

8 644   B–Kt5 $\dfrac{\text{Kt–Q5}}{\text{Kt–B5}}$ $\underline{\text{Kt} \times \text{B}}$

Ah well, $\dfrac{\text{Kt} \times \text{Q}}{\text{B} \times \text{P mate}}$ was a good try!

578   B–K3 $\dfrac{\text{Kt–Q5}}{\text{B} \times \text{Kt}}$ $\underline{\text{P} \times \text{B}}$

Why does it reject a variation which allows mate in 2?

$\underline{564}$ P–B3 $\dfrac{\text{0–0–0}}{\text{B–Kt5}}$ $\underline{\text{P–B3}}$

9 $\underline{809}$ Kt–Kt5 $\dfrac{\text{P–B3}}{\text{Kt–K6}}$ $\underline{\text{B–Q3}}$

781   Kt–Kt3 $\dfrac{\text{0–0–0}}{\text{P–B4}}$ $\underline{\text{B–Q3}}$

715   Kt–B2 $\dfrac{\text{0–0–0}}{\text{Kt–Kt4}}$ $\underline{\text{B–Q3}}$

10 557   KKt–R3 $\dfrac{\text{P–KR3}}{\text{B} \times \text{Kt}}$ $\dfrac{\text{B} \times \text{B}}{\text{Q–K3}}$ $\dfrac{\text{P–Q5}}{\text{Q} \times \text{KP}}$

$\dfrac{\text{R–K1}}{\text{Kt-K6}}$ $\text{R} \times \text{Kt}$

557   B–K3 $\dfrac{\text{P–Q5}}{\text{B–Q2}}$ $\dfrac{\text{B–K2}}{\text{B} \times \text{Kt}}$ $\dfrac{\text{B} \times \text{B}}{\text{Q} \times \text{P}}$

$\underline{548}$ B–Q2 $\dfrac{\text{P–KR3}}{\text{QKt–R3}}$ $\dfrac{\text{P–R3}}{\text{B–R4}}$ $\underline{\text{B–B4}}$

11 $\underline{846}$ QKt–R3 $\dfrac{\text{Q–K3}}{\text{0–0–0}}$ $\dfrac{\text{P–Q5}}{\text{B–QB4}}$ $\underline{\text{Q–B3}}$

765   KKt–R3 $\dfrac{\text{P–KR3}}{\text{B} \times \text{Kt}}$ $\underline{\text{B} \times \text{B}}$

729   P–KR4 $\dfrac{\text{P–KR3}}{\text{P–R5}}$ $\underline{\text{Q–B3}}$

12 $\underline{656}$ P–Kt3 $\dfrac{\text{B–B3}}{\text{0–0–0}}$ $\underline{\text{KKt–K2}}$

499   Kt–B2 $\dfrac{\text{Q} \times \text{KtP}}{\text{B} \times \text{Kt}}$ $\underline{\text{Q} \times \text{R}}$

352	K–B1	$\dfrac{\text{KKt–K2}}{\text{P–KKt3}}$	B–B3	

13 768	0–0–0	$\dfrac{\text{P–KR4}}{\text{R–K1}}$	$\dfrac{\text{P–R5}}{\text{P–KKt4}}$	KKt–K2?

564	P–KB4	$\dfrac{\text{P–Q5}}{\text{Kt–B3}}$	$\dfrac{\text{P}\times\text{QBP}}{\text{KtP}\times\text{P}}$

563	P–QB4	$\dfrac{\text{Kt–Q5}}{\text{Q–K3}}$	Kt–B7 ch.

No wonder this variation was rejected.

14 768	0–0–0	$\dfrac{\text{P–Q5}}{\text{Kt–B3}}$	$\dfrac{\text{P}\times\text{QBP}}{\text{KtP}\times\text{P}}$

701	Kt–B3	$\dfrac{\text{P–K5}}{\text{KKt–Kt5}}$	$\dfrac{\text{P}\times\text{P}}{\text{B}\times\text{P}}$	Kt–B4

532	B×Kt	$\dfrac{\text{B}\times\text{B}}{\text{P}\times\text{P}}$	$\dfrac{\text{P–Q5}}{\text{Kt–B2}}$	$\dfrac{\text{B–K2}}{\text{Kt–B3}}$
		$\dfrac{\text{Kt–B4}}{\text{P}\times\text{P}}$	Kt×QP	

B×Kt was in fact the 7th highest marked move in the first investigation.

15 865	P×P	$\dfrac{\text{B}\times\text{P}}{\text{Kt–B4}}$	$\dfrac{\text{Q–B3}}{\text{P–Q4}}$	B–Q3

768	0–0–0	$\dfrac{\text{P–K5}}{\text{P}\times\text{P}}$	Q×P

621	Kt–B3	$\dfrac{\text{P–K5}}{\text{Kt–R4}}$	Q–Kt5

16 1210	Q×B	$\dfrac{\text{KR–K1}}{\text{Q–K2}}$	$\dfrac{\text{R}\times\text{Q ch.}}{\text{K}\times\text{R}}$

830	Kt–B4	$\dfrac{\text{Q–B3}}{\text{P–Q4}}$	$\dfrac{\text{B–Q3}}{\text{Q–R6}}$	$\dfrac{\text{K–Q2}}{\text{Q}\times\text{RP?}}$

On Move 15, Kt–B4 was preferred to Q×B, as will be seen in the first line.

768	0–0–0	$\dfrac{\text{B–Q3}}{\text{Kt–B4}}$	Q–B3

<u>677</u> P–Q4 B–Q3 / Q–R6 B–Kt2 / Q×P

P–Q4 was the 6th highest move at first.

17 1002 P×B QR–K1 / B–K3 Q×P ch. / K–Q2 Kt–B4 / R–KB1 Kt×B / R×P

515 Kt–B2 B×P / Kt–Kt4 Kt×Kt / R×B

<u>348</u> K–B1 Q–B4 ch. / K–Kt2 B–Q3 / Q–R6 B–Kt2 / Q×P

18 1002 P×B B–R3 / Kt–B4 B×Q ch. / KKt×B

880 Kt–B4 B×Kt / B×B B–R3 / P–B4 <u>B×P</u>

<u>563</u> Q–B3 Q–B7 / P×B Q×B / P–Kt3 B–R3 ch. / Kt–K2

Q–B3 was the 9th highest move at first.

19 624 · K–K2 B–R5 / Kt–B4 Q–B7 / B–B1

540 K–Kt2 B–B5 dis. ch. / K–B2 <u>B×B</u>

361 P–B4 B×P ch. / Kt–K2 <u>B–R5</u>

20 1354 Kt–B4 B×Kt / Q×B <u>B×Kt ch.</u>

1218 P×B B×Kt ch. / Q×B R×Q / K×R <u>Q×P</u>

919 Kt–Kt1 B–R5 / B–K3 P–KB4 / Q–B4 <u>B–B3</u>

21 1180 P×B Kt×P ch. / K–B2 Kt×Kt / Q–R3 ch. R–K3 / Kt×Kt

B×Kt / Q×P Q×Q / R×Q

744 P–B4 B×BP / P–Kt3 B×Kt ch. / Kt×B

<u>536</u>	R–B1	$\dfrac{\text{B–R5}}{\text{B–B4}}$	$\dfrac{\text{B–B5}}{\text{P–Kt3}}$	<u>B–QKt4</u>
22 <u>1972</u>	Kt×R	$\dfrac{\text{R–K1}}{\text{P–B4}}$	$\dfrac{\text{B×BP}}{\text{P×B (a)}}$	<u>B×Kt ch.</u>
or	Kt×R	$\dfrac{\text{R–K1}}{\text{P–B4}}$	$\dfrac{\text{B×BP}}{\text{P×B (a)}}$	$\dfrac{\text{Q–K3}}{\text{K–B2}}$
		$\dfrac{\text{Q×Kt ch.}}{\text{Q×Q}}$	<u>R×Q ch.</u>	

(a) Two variations, but neither giving R×B!

1220	P×B	$\dfrac{\text{R×B dis. ch.}}{\text{K–K1}}$	<u>R–Q6</u>	
944	R–B2	$\dfrac{\text{R–B7 d. ch.}}{\text{K–K1}}$	$\dfrac{\text{R×Q dis. ch.}}{\text{P×B}}$	
23 1180	P×B	$\dfrac{\text{B×Kt ch.}}{\text{Q×B}}$	$\dfrac{\text{Kt×P ch.}}{\text{K–B2}}$	<u>Kt×Q</u>
<u>776</u>	P–B4	$\dfrac{\text{Q–K3}}{\text{P–Kt3}}$	$\dfrac{\text{B–Q3}}{\text{Kt–B4}}$	$\dfrac{\text{B×Kt}}{\text{B×B}}$ <u>Kt×P</u>
626	Q×P	$\dfrac{\text{B×Kt ch.}}{\text{K–Kt2}}$	<u>Kt–K6 ch.</u>	

Index of Openings

Caro-Kann Defence 24
Catalan System 35, 57
English Opening 54
Evans Gambit 33
French Defence 5
Giuoco Piano 60
King's Gambit 30, 55
King's Gambit Declined 23
Petroff Defence 51
Pirc Defence 14, 54
Polish Opening 73
Queen's Gambit Declined:
  Cambridge Springs 25
  Orthodox Defence 49
  Slav Defence 9, 52

Queen's Pawn:
  Benoni Defence 28
  Queen's Indian Defence 27
Ruy Lopez:
  Closed Defence 48, 53
  Möller Defence 64, 67, 69, 70 (2)
Sicilian Defence 11 (2), 47, 50
  2 P-QB3 41, 42, 43, 44, 45, 46
  Wing Gambit 38, 39 (2), 40
Two Knights Defence 59
Vienna Gambit 58
Vienna Game 32, 56 (2)

Index of Players

Adams 32
Aitken 52
Alekhine 64, 67 (2), 69
Barker 33
Basman 44
Bird, R. 5
Blackburne 23
Bolland 62
Bruce 57
Capablanca 69
Clarke 70
Collins 41
Combe 61
Cook, J. 11
Corden 63
Cvachoucek 45
Euwe 30
Gibbs 54
Gray 56
Green 54
Guimard 27
Herrick 9
Hindle 40
Hollis 39
Keene 14
Kitto 58
Machack VI 73
Markwell 60
Marshall, W. 33
Michell 49

Milner-Barry 55, 67, 69
Müller 61
Najdorf 28
Northage 59
Oddie 11
Oppenheim 8
Parr 50
Penrose 14, 48, 62
Pritchard 51
Reti 24
Rothbart 11
Rubinstein 25
Schmidt 56
Sergeant 53, 70, 71
Shipley and Sharp 67
'Smith', L. 39
Spencer 3
Spiller 47
Steiner 69
Stonier 9
Takacs 67
Tartakower 35
Tylor 38
Unzicker 33
Walker, P. 5
Williams 11
Wood 43
Woodward 42
Yates 64
Zehnder 46